Climb The Joyous Mountain

Climb the Joyous Mountain

Living the Meditative Way

by
JUSTIN F. STONE

GOOD KARMA
Fort Yates
1992

GOOD KARMA PUBLISHING, Inc., Publisher
P.O. Box 511
Fort Yates, ND 58538

Printed in the United States of America

First Good Karma Publishing, Inc. edition - 1992

Text printed on recycled paper

Library of Congress Catalog Card Number 90-82709

ISBN 0-9620812-5-6

DEDICATED TO
MY MOTHER, ANNE, WITH
THANKS FOR THE PATIENCE
SHOWN DURING THE DIFFICULT
YEARS.

Climbing,

Climbing,

Climbing —

finally

we

hit . . . .

bottom!

TABLE OF CONTENTS

FOREWORD

Justin Stone is an authentic spiritual teacher. His is a remarkable non-preaching teaching! Justin's true teaching is continually reflected and effortlessly demonstrated in the way he lives.

Justin enthusiastically conducts seminars and delivers brilliantly informative lectures in order to fulfill his students' requests. He has authored several spiritual books that offer inspiration and practical direction. He is also a gifted painter and musician. Justin is a man of many talents and accomplishments, which hints at the quantity and quality of creative energy flowing through him. Beyond all his wonderful capabilities and engaging personality, Justin Stone is an unusually rare kind of teacher. He is one who *lives* the spiritual life. And though his life appears to be quite ordinary in many ways, when rightly understood, it is recognized as extraordinary and deeply profound.

We are fortunate to have this current edition of *Climb the Joyous Mountain*, originally published in 1975. It presents a vitally significant spiritual message, in very human terms, through Justin's distinctive and compassionate voice.

In Chapter One, we are privileged to share in a meditation experience of Justin's through his sensitive description. He explains the preparatory breathing technique, the resulting internal process, and the aftermath state of renewed perception. His use of personal and warmly poetic word pictures helps give us a tangible idea of meditative awareness. In another chapter, we accompany Justin on a meaningful and subtly inspiring adventure through his favorite Japanese city. He also explains the Japanese concept called "Wabi Sabi," related to the refined sense of appreciation for nature and art in the context of paintings, flower arrangements, pottery, gardens and various structures.

Justin's moving description of his silent encounter with a God-intoxicated holy man in India is unique and inspiring. In fact, he favors us with numerous stories, both humorous and serious, of his travels through old-world countries. The stories serve as poignant reminders of spirituality and are meaningful observations for purposeful contemplation.

Justin states his views on Chinese Taoism, Indian Buddhism and other approaches to spirituality. He clearly and decisively explains the "meaning of suffering" and describes the inherent tendencies and inadequacies of the "human condition," while suggesting possible antidotes.

This book contains substantial spiritual messages that help remind us of the proper and advantageous relationship we can have with life. Justin reveals, with a flavor of obviousness and candor, that ours can be an existence of continuing creative expression and joyous enrichment, if we so decide.

Justin's apt title, *Climb the Joyous Mountain*, admonishes and challenges us to earnestly begin our quest for true self-understanding and fulfillment. Climbing a mountain is an appropriate metaphor for embarking on the journey of spiritual remembrance. We aspire to attain the ultimate satisfaction of living wholly, of actualizing our deepest potentials, through a persistent effort to overcome all that seems to restrict us.

This uphill path is arduous and difficult until we come to the point where we are able to discern that actually, we have always been "That" which we have been attempting to apprehend! What we truly are, at the core of our existence, prompts our spiritual journey so that It may realize full expression through the mind-body. The spiritual quest is nothing more than the conscious act of encountering and resolving the self-created limitations we have superimposed upon our "core nature." Our core nature or essential identity is ever joyous. Justin explains this fact by stating, "Joy is your natural state, though it is usually covered over. When the Mind returns to its natural condition (free of restrictive conditionings), you are joyful."

At the foundation of our challenging mountain of difficulties lies pure Joy. May we traverse this mountain of promise skillfully, as we symbolically climb toward our lofty spiritual aspirations, until we joyously hit bottom! Perhaps it is from this foundation that our true spiritual odyssey begins.

Steve Ridley
March 17, 1992
Denver, CO

INTRODUCTION

There is, in this writer, a sense of unworthiness about writing a book called "Climb the Joyous Mountain." One time, when I mentioned the many errors in my life to the Bengali teacher, Rammurti Mishra, he immediately snapped: "Those are not your mistakes!" This is really distinguishing the Unreal from the Real, and I am grateful to him for the profound lesson, though the sense of unworthiness insanely persists.

It seems that much of my adult life has seen me the fortunate recipient of such lessons. When the wife of Zen Priest Ogata gave me a Zen lecture by saying: "Stone san!" and then slowly letting her folded fist open and unfold as a flower unfolds, it made me want to cry. Surely she is one of the world's great women!

Her husband, who spoke such excellent English, once said to me: "Anybody can be the Small Hermit. Be the Big Hermit!" Much later, meditating in the foothills of the Himalayas, I thought of this and said to myself: "What am I doing up here, being the Small Hermit? I should be able to do this at the corner of Broadway and 42nd St.!" So I am grateful for these two lessons.

Always there has been a dichotomy in my mind between the necessity of earning money on which to live and a shrinking-back at selling somebody something so that I could profit by it. In Music, all that was wanted was a chance to Express, but, for some years in the Stock Market, I tried to put aside my reluctance and play by the Rules of the Game. There was some "success," too, but it was meaningless. Accumulation of money could not compensate for going against my own Flow. And yet, we must work to live. The Buddha spoke of "Right Livelihood," and what is right for me might be wrong for another. How can we tell another what to do? We can ask meaningful questions, and we can offer a constructive example, but we cannot define another's life. To try to live what I AM, this seems to make sense. Often, in the eyes of others, it makes us look like fools. It is funny that, even today, when I dream, it is usually about the period of my life in Music. I have never dreamt about the Stock Market.

The anecdotes in this book are not there for the purpose of Reminiscence. Rather, they point, for me, in the direction of "The Joyous Mountain." A leap in the air, clicking the heels, or a really delighted laugh will beat all the torturous discussion, without a doubt. And still we write books!

Does writing books make me a writer? I don't know. Does writing about the "Joyous Mountain" make one joyous? I don't know. So, what do I know? Well, there have been moments at the piano when the Music flowed like T'ai Chi Ch'uan, and moments of grace in athletics. But Sports are competitive – and I was very competitive! – and competition can be murderous. Looking back at some moments in the Orient, when I was just fortunate to be at a particular place, I realize how rich the Fabric is. After Meditation, some times, we feel an inexpressible thankfulness. For What? To Whom?

All one can do is bring his palms together in a salute to All Beings. May they lose the attachment that makes for suffering! Life *can* be good – if we plant the proper seeds. The Way of Joy is best! Climb the Joyous Mountain!

Preamble

This commentary was suggested by the painter, OU MIE SHU whose fine works are seen later in this book. It was written by HAN YU during the TANG Dynasty in China (roughly 600-900 A. D.).

GENERALLY SPEAKING, EVERYTHING SINGS BECAUSE OF BEING ABUSED. GRASS AND WOODS HAVE NO SOUND; THEY SING ONLY WHEN THE WIND INTERFERES. WATER HAS NO SOUND OF ITS OWN; IT IS THE WIND THAT MAKES IT SING. IT IS JUMPING, SKIPPING, RUNNING ONLY BECAUSE IT WAS DRIVEN, STOPPED, OR HEATED. STONE HAS NO SOUND; IT SINGS ONLY WHEN IT IS BEATEN.

SPEECH WITH MAN IS THE SAME. HE SPEAKS ONLY BECAUSE HE HAS TO. THERE ARE THOUGHTS IN HIS SONG AND HE TELLS HIS STORY WHEN HE CRIES. WHATEVER SOUNDS COME OUT OF THE MOUTH MUST ALL HAVE THEIR REASONS. MUSIC, SO TO SPEAK, IS THE SOUND EXPRESSED WITHOUT FROM WHAT'S WITHIN. AND IT CHOOSES THE BEST INSTRUMENTS TO SING FOR ITS SOUL. METAL, STONE, STRING, BAMBOO, EARTHENWARE, LEATHER, WOOD, PIPES ARE THE CAPABLE SINGERS FOR NATURE (THE CHINESE BELIEVE THE INTERNAL ORGANS HAVE AN URGE TO EXPRESS. ONLY THE PROPER INSTRUMENTS RELATED TO THE INTERNAL ORGANS CAN EXTEND AND EXPRESS THEIR NEED IN MUSIC).

SO NATURE TREATS ITS SEASONS, CHOOSES ITS MOST SKILLFUL SINGERS TO EXPRESS THE TIME OF YEAR. BIRDS HAVE BEEN SENT TO SING IN SPRING, THUNDER FOR SUMMER, INSECTS FOR AUTUMN, AND WINDS IN WINTER. THE FOUR SEASONS PUSH EACH OTHER ON. EACH EXPRESSES ALL CREATION WITH ITS COMPLAINTS IN SONG.

Climb
the
Joyous
Mountain

CHAPTER 1

LIVING THE MEDITATIVE WAY

It had been a cool morning. Expectedly, there had been a number of phone calls—one from a student who asked if he could make up the Meditation class he had missed, one from an older woman who had vague psychological problems, and several from strangers who had viewed the Television interview on the Educational Channel a few nights before (my number was not hard to find in the phone book). Now the mind, accustomed to a formal meditation period at this time, began to drift in that direction. I glanced at the clock and was surprised to note that it was 11 A. M. already.

Quickly I slipped out the back door and went to where my car was parked in the shade. Opening the door and slipping inside, I had already put the world and daily events out of my mind. That afternoon and evening would be very active, but, at the moment, I was dedicated to entering the "natural" state, beyond thought, and impossible to describe to those who have not experienced it. In truth, of course, there is no-one to enter such a state, and, in another sense, we are always in it. But these are just words. I settled back in the seat, still keeping the backbone firm.

Closing my eyes, I slowly moved the warm feeling from the small of my back to the base of the skull, then took it to the top of the head. As I did so, I inhaled, and retained the breath as the light reached the apex of the circle. Then, with the breath held in, I mentally repeated the Mantra (sound, or sounds, that are the Name of God) several times. As I gradually exhaled, I brought the light down the front, past the face, neck, and abdomen, until it reached the spot two inches below the navel (which the Chinese call the T'an T'ien). Then, with the breath entirely expelled, I rested quietly in the emptiness. I had been careful to breathe out slowly and in sections, as though lowering to different levels, and, when I had reached what seemed to be bottom, I breathed out once more. This obviated the need for the reflex in-breath, which, otherwise, would have occurred immediately. Resting in the emptiness of the T'an T'ien, without breath, there was the feeling that one could stay there all day. In a minute or two, however, I would once again start the Great Circle as I took the light through the opening between the legs and, once again, slowly up the channel in the back.

The exaggerated in-breathing and out-breathing that accompanied the course of the light were accomplished in what I call the Meditative Breathing way, which is just opposite to what we normally do. When breathing in, the abdomen and chest expanded, and stayed so while the Mantra was being inserted. As I then brought the light down and exhaled, the abdomen and chest contracted, the anus was pulled in tight, and the stomach was finally plastered tight against the backbone as the last air was pushed out. The body looked thinnest as I rested in the T'an T'ien, and the tightened anus kept the air from escaping down below, as I gradually let out the large amount of oxygen through the nostrils. This type of Meditative Breathing can, itself, take one into deep meditation.

After three or four of these great circles, with the mental meditation of the Mantra while the in-breath was held, the Mind went completely quiet. Then I resumed normal breathing, and began to mentally count the out-breaths, which came very slowly. "One, two, three," I counted, and then seemed to move into a different level of consciousness. The counting stopped, the breathing almost stopped, and there were no thoughts. Neither the world, its inhabitants, nor its ideas existed. There was only an awareness hard to describe—and there was no object in this awareness. Perhaps the Buddhist word *Tathata*—roughly translated as "Suchness"—would be the best description. There was a livingness and an awareness, but no-one who was doing the living and no-one to be aware and nothing to be aware of! Time passed rapidly and imperceptibly in this state.

Occasionally, I would slip back to normal thinking, and would immediately begin counting again. Without pause, the thoughtless state of pure consciousness would be reassumed. Ten minutes or an hour, it was hard to tell how much time was passing.

Suddenly, almost violently, I was hurled out of this state and back into the world. Totally disconnected thoughts were the first sign of re-emergence, and I felt I could actually watch the mind recreating the world around me. Somehow, I knew the Meditation was over—the mind had had enough.

Still, I sat there quietly. There was no urge to move, to do something; to be was enough. The mind, having tasted the bliss of one-pointedness, reached through introspection, was in no hurry to turn outward again and scatter itself. The one-pointed mind is strong, and the restless one is the cause of untold suffering.

Idly I noted how green were the leaves of the trees, standing tall against the deep blue cloudless sky. The symbolism was not lost on me. It was much like the famous Haiku of the Japanese poet, Basho, when the stillness of the pond is rudely pierced by the "splash" of the frog as he dives in. The swaying motion of the leaves contrasted with the infinite stillness of deep blue we call sky—life moving incomprehensibly against the nothingness of the void. How does there come to be this movement? Who has ordained it? But the mind, still and at oneness, has no desire to tackle such problems. To be is the thing, at the moment, and questions have no place in such stillness.

The Japanese speak of "seijaku," the deep stillness that is within activity. Their ideal is not to isolate themselves, as the Indians do, but to experience this stillness in each moment of activity, to taste the Bliss of Being even while, momentarily, experiencing disappointment. As I sat there, I knew the rest of the day would be busy. There would be three classes, sandwiched around a cross-legged Zen Meditation sitting (Zazen), lasting up to nine o'clock that night at which time I would drive a few of my wheel-less T'ai Chi students home and then prepare tea for a few young friends who wanted to come by and talk. But the current generated by this period of immersion (my watch showed about forty-five minutes had passed) would last all day, later buttressed by the hour period of Zen sitting, quite different in scope and effect from the deep meditation I had just practised. And, of course, early in the morning I had performed T'ai Chi Ch'uan and T'ai Chi Chih in the backyard, followed by some Zen sitting and chanting of the Heart Sutra. These activities had become natural to me. They were not compulsion, but something I deeply looked forward to.

Leaving the car, I again noted how green the trees were. There was something coursing through me, not like the flow of Chi from T'ai Chi Ch'uan, but a thing indescribable. I vaguely remembered that something had been worrying me before Meditation, but I could not recall the details. A problem that had been in the back of my mind for weeks now stood forth boldly, and it was plain to see that the answer was encompassed in the problem itself. Most problems now seemed to exist only on an oral level. Living the meditative way had removed the need for soul-searching and self-doubting. Things were as they were, and it was easy to flow with them. And this strange pulsing within reminded me, once more, of the poet's lines about the flying geese high above the pond at sunset—"there is a meaning to all this, but, when I get to this point, I become lost in no-words."

It is said that "to the mind that is still, the Universe surrenders." It is not easy to make the monkey-mind still, and it cannot be forced to be so. Those Yogis who try to forcibly restrain the mind are on the wrong track; hold out the Bliss of the thoughtless state to the mind and, as it becomes used to it, it will go there with no effort, making it possible to once again be Yourself. The stillness is always there, and the Universe is always ready to surrender.

Such formal periods of Meditation are not always possible. At other times, it is feasible to sit cross-legged within the house, remembering to take the phone off the hook. Meditation can be anywhere, but the mind must be trained. The Universe does not surrender to the scattered mind. As Sister Carita is supposed to have written: "Don't just do something; stand there." How nice to be Ourselves! To make effort without effort, this is the trick. And this is why we meditate.

Re-entering the house, I heard the telephone's incessant ring. Not wishing to honor its harsh demand, I ignored it. Instead, I chose a Palestrina record from a small pile and played the Church music I had been indifferent to before. This time it was different. Subconsciously, deep levels of feeling opened inside and the religious message was conveyed. When it came time for lunch, I played the other side. Irrelevantly, the music reminded me of a time I visited a Temple for Pregnant Snakes on the Malaysian

Island of Penang. Perhaps it was a remembrance of the lush green undergrowth there, awakened by the overpowering green of the trees after my meditation, that brought back such a memory. There is stillness everywhere; perhaps we only imagine the noise. There is no confusion among pregnant snakes, and Palestrina only made sense at this time, not logical, but a-logical sense. I remembered one time, after a long meditation, sitting at a piano and improvising, and having the feeling that somebody else was playing and I was only listening. This was like watching the movements of T'ai Chi Ch'uan do themselves, with one's self just an observer—observing whom? Stalagmites and stalagtites—which were which? Somehow, all were enclosed in the music, and the music was my meditation, which had never ended. With no-one to talk to, the mind was shut off—there was no need to get lost in "no words." From such wordless times comes the greatest creativity. Re-charging the batteries, we pour forth a current of creative doing, and yet it is not ours. I remembered how I had once felt, instinct-ively, that "each is singing the Glory of Creation." Had there really been a Creation? That question, posed to an Indian wise man, had brought forth the answer, "It's hard to tell." When we go deep within ourselves, the answers do not come; rather the questions are removed. How much more glorious the trip into Inner Space—and how much vaster! We have a telescope with which to look outward on the Universe. Where is its opposite number, that will enable us to go within? With such a telescope the scientist could not only look at the outer reaches of space, millions of light years away, but, more important, would begin to understand who it is that is looking. In this way we climb the Joyous Mountain—and, climbing, climbing, finally we hit Bottom.

There are, of course, those who argue that no formal medi-tation is necessary, that there is no need for any discipline whatever. These are often people who drink, smoke pot, and titillate the senses in various ways. With the insatiable mind demanding more and more diversion, they turn to narcotics of various forms (end-less diversion is a narcotic), thereby deadening the mind and dulling the awareness. Naturally, they speak against self-culture. But the great Zen Master, Dogen Zenji, founder of the Soto Zen sect in Japan, flatly stated: "There is no enlightenment without practice."

So the self-proclaimed independents find no support from me. From them we get books about T'ai Chi by those who have never practised T'ai Chi, and treatises on Zen and Yoga by those who have never practised Zen and Yoga. We are in a world that loves "ersatz," so it is not hard to interest people in reading about the "essence" of some discipline by one who has never experienced it.

Exercise develops the muscles. Concentration strengthens the mind. It is useless to talk of "devotion" and "non-attachment" unless the mind is capable of one-pointed concentration, which has nothing to do with intellectual attainment. One scholar reads what another scholar has written, and then, himself, writes a book using the diffused (and confused) information. One such Ph.D., a much-honored instructor in a University Philosophy Department, found she was the only one in a large class of undergraduates who could not learn or execute T'ai Chi Ch'uan! This was a great blow to the ego, so she dropped it. It is not surprising to hear talk of suicide from such a one, in whom the great teachings of the Buddha have not made the slightest dent.

In truth, only an enlightened one can really practise Devotion. We do not practise it and then become enlightened. Yet the mind—and the nervous system—must be cultured. There is no doubt the Truth lies within us—we *are* the truth. But, to know it and manifest it is a different matter. If we would live the meditative way, we must meditate. The current of constant meditation will gradually pervade the whole life, and each action will, in itself, be "pure." We are all Saints in embryo, and we are all Divine. To go within and merge with this Divinity, to flow with the current of the Life Force, is not so easy until we have fasted and fasted in the sense that Chuang-Tzu meant when he spoke of the "Fasting Mind." Any blithe talk of "I understand what you mean"—as though listening to a sermon will concentrate the unsteady mind—and any feeling that "I know the essence, so I don't really have to practise it" are cop-outs. Perhaps, after twenty years of repeating the Nembutsu (Hail to the Buddha of Infinite Light—Namu Amida Butsu), the sincere Jodo Shinshu believer finds this Mantra constantly echoed in his heart, so it does not matter whether or not he phrases it with the lips. But there have been twenty years of one-pointed practice! "Satori" is not a word to be used loosely by those who think it is some sort of momentary satisfaction experienced after a good meal. We plant seeds and eventually reap the fruit; an apple seed brings only an apple tree, and from it we do not derive watermelons.

To know quiescence in the midst of activity is more than tranquilization. Peace is not merely a "blotting-out." If we are willing to pay the price, we receive the reward. In such a way we can rise to true Human status. Otherwise we remain mere animals eating, sleeping, and suffering. Remember we make the choice.

When at the end of the Tenrikyo Church ceremonies, I have heard the simple devotees shout "Joyous Life!", in what, for them, is a foreign tongue, I have felt a warmth within. With the constant discipline of their impressive services, I have no doubt many have reached a one-pointed stage. The doctrine itself is of no importance. Such faith and devotion cultures the "Heart-Mind-Spirit" (Kokoro), and what a man believes is not as important as the fact of his truly believing it. Religion is full of contradictions. Religiosity may well exist without formal religion. An inner sincerity and a constant practise of what is believed must succeed. Meditation is one way down this road, though not the only way.

Does a flower live a meditative life? I do not know. Under the snow, perhaps, the plum blossom rests in meditation, until it is time to send forth shoots and bring the delicious fruit to fulfillment. A solitary plant growing insanely from seemingly barren rock expresses a great and indomitable life force. To be aware of such a life force, to walk serenely beneath the awesome blue sky, and to listen to the spring raindrops on the overhanging eaves of the old temple building–these are all meditative experiences if we merge into them.

"At first I thought it was frost on the cold wooden floor," says the poet. "Then I realized it was the full moon shining through the window of my small cabin. Seeing the bright, reflected light, I thought of my home far away." Sad? Not really. Reflective, retrospective, making us more aware of what is within us as a reaction to what is without–and knowing that the outside, our world around us, is a reflection of the inner. To rest in such a moment is, itself, tranquil, though we may never see our home again. We all die, in the sense that the body disintegrates. Indeed, in one sense we are dying from the day we are born. But, in the larger sense, awareness expanding makes us more and more alive, until we merge in the Pure Consciousness that knows no death. Think of the Pure Consciousness as fathomless Blue Sky. This is neither positive nor negative, and meditation lies between the two poles.

The mirror-mind accurately reflects, and what it reflects is true, unconditioned by sentiment and opinion. The sudden squall is neither good nor bad, and, when felt in its absolute value that brooks no duality, it is merely what it is. When the storm is over, the clouds break and the sun shines once more. We know that, behind the clouds, it has never ceased to shine.

The 108 movements of T'ai Chi Ch'uan are, too, a meditation. One day, while practising, we suddenly feel as though no-one is doing this ancient Chinese discipline, that the movements are moving of themselves and we are merely observers. It is an ecstatic feeling, born of long practice. The involuntary trembling in the fingers, resulting from the flowing "CHI" energy, surprises us at first; it is not of our doing, and we do not control it. This flow of infinite energy is greater than "ourselves." Coming from nowhere, going nowhere, it is just there, and we learn to rest in it. Old people in Taiwan and China, swinging back and forth in a relaxed manner in what they call "The Dharma Tendon-Building movement," feel tensions drop away as the Vital Force flows through the system. "What lovely Ikebana:" we exclaim when we see the unselfconscious flower arrangement the Japanese Master has wrought. "Yes," he acknowledges. "They all grew near here."

CHAPTER 2

COLD KYOTO MORNING

It is always cold when we arise at 5:30 A. M. on a winter's morning in Kyoto. If I am staying at the small Tenrikyo church community, just off Karasuma Street—near the ancient Emperor's Palace—there is a good deal of noise and bustling at the start of the day. Children are dressed for school, old women clean the floors of the latrines, and those who work in the large kitchen begin to get the rice and Miso soup ready to feed forty people the first meal of the day. The activity will slacken about 7 A. M., when the Dawn Service begins in the Main Sanctuary. Then will come breakfast, and everybody will be busy through the day until the Sunset Service, unless there is a special Ceremonial Occasion.

With no central heating system to ward off the cruel winds in Kyoto, the cold is piercing. Nevertheless, by custom, most windows are opened wide at morning. If I am cold in my heavy winter underwear, as I leave the Futon (bedroll), so is everybody else; consequently, it is not so bad. When we do not suffer alone, we do not really suffer.

Just before Morning Service we slip into the kitchen to place our frozen hands over the huge cauldron of Miso soup. The flame underneath sends up a pleasing heat, and there is a chance to thaw the fingers. When I do T'ai Chi Ch'uan in the lovely garden, near the tea-house, I usually wear gloves, though they certainly restrict the freedom of motion. In the early morning stillness, before the late winter sun has risen, there is a stark silence that penetrates one's being. The last stars disappear from view, but the pale moon remains for some time. The inevitable mind-wandering stops suddenly as the Bang! of the big bass drum begins the preliminaries of the Service. If it is the day of a special ceremony, the sound of ancient Chinese flutes can be heard coming from the Main Sanctuary. T'ai Chi at an end, I hurry there for the Service.

The faces of the old people, as they chant, sing, and pirouette in their ritual dance, tell me of what is going on inside them. A Japanese Zen scholar, who visited me there, said that the utter sincerity brought tears to his eyes. Such steadfastness, such unquestioning faith, must be very pleasing to the Tenrikyo God. After the final words have been chanted, in a sort of responsive reading, an old man with a beautiful face catches my eye, smiles, and points to his heart. "Kokoro," he murmurs softly, the all-inclusive word for "Heart–Mind–Spirit" that does not indicate the physical organ but something much deeper. The younger people do not seem to derive the same benefits, however. They are anxious to finish the hour-long ceremony and get on with the day's living, or so it seems to me.

The simple breakfast that follows the service is not very fitting; some rice, a few cold vegetables, and the bean paste soup known as Miso. The cold gives everyone a good appetite, however. Later in the morning, the more privileged ministers (who have been up late the night before) will drift in, a few for western-style scrambled eggs (cold before it reaches them) and toast. I ask if I can have an apple, and the request is passed along to 89-year-old Obaasan, the great-grandmother Matriarch of the establishment. Of course she smiles her assent. We are good friends, and, in the steaming hot summer, she combats the humidity by going naked from the waist up, despite the presence of me, the foreigner; no other woman dares do that. When she grants permission, one of the kitchen women sets to work laboriously peeling and slicing the delicious ringo, the Japanese apple, for me. This may be the same lady I woke the night before, when I came home late through the dark alleys and found it necessary to ring the bell at the outer gate. There is no resentment on her face, however, as she beams at me and hands me a plate with the apple on it. I wonder if she's the one who sometimes slips a glass of juice into the outer room of the Ofuro (Japanese bath) while I am bathing; one gets quite thirsty in the very hot water the Japanese love so much.

The cold is a frequent topic of conversation in winter. Schoolgirls walking arm-in-arm to school, wearing blue middy blouses, smile and chatter "samui, samui!" as they step off the streetcars. They have good reason to be cold; they don't wear coats! No chance of this generation going soft. Grandmothers carrying babies on their backs hustle along the streets, softly whispering "samui, samui!" to the little ones, so bundled up that nothing but tiny faces can be seen peeking out of the grandma's outer garments.

"Samu narimashita!" says the woman cleaning the latrine, lapsing into Kyoto dialect. Any such smart answer as "It's always cold in winter" would not be comprehended. The correct reply is a simple repetition of the same phrase, spoken in a surprised tone of voice.

Most Japanese eat meboshi, the sour plum that prevents the constipation attendant upon a diet of such soft food. However, the bitter taste of meboshi and the smell of soy sauce do not appeal to the westerner at the cold breakfast table, and one must find another way to keep the stomach in order.

When I have spent winters at the Zen sub-temple nearby, the cold is even more accentuated by the presence of an inner garden. As one pads along the hallway to the latrine, he passes a small inner garden opening onto the hallway, with not even the thin shoji screens keeping out the chill of the snow and ice on the ground. The temple people *could* screen off the small garden, but the aesthetic sense is stronger than the fear of the cold, and it is left because it is pleasing. And, once one has admitted the cold and accepted it, there is nothing more to say about it. When one walks out the front gate of the main temple building, in the frozen moonlight, there is an unearthly halo around the trees and an air of vibrant stillness that penetrates deep down inside. A walk along the graveled path is an adventure, and one forgets the poor frozen ego in favor of something greater. Behind these trees are buried 700 years of monks—some heroes, some weak and unable to penetrate the heights of Zen. All have meditated at midnight in that freezing cold, no covering on their feet and ankles. Sometimes, lying in the warm Futon in the middle of the night, I would hear the chanting begin—"Maka Hanya Haramita Shin Gyo!"—and I would think, "the poor bastards!"

But, of course, I didn't mean it. To follow such a way without doubt is to be inculcated with a discipline and a belief that ignores such discomforts. And the reward is far greater than can be imagined.

Nowhere else have I seen the lavender skies of Kyoto. When there is winter snow—which doesn't last long—the clouds form a covering somewhat like black-and-white Sumi-e paintings, and the hills that ring Kyoto (politely called "mountains") are sometimes lost in mist. At such a time I like to climb to the "Philosopher's Path" (Tetsugakusha no Michi) on the Eastern mountain, from where I can see much of the city spread below. It is a good time to visit temples, as they are not too crowded in inclement weather. Afterwards, a visit to a favorite coffee-house seems indicated, to drink the delicious and outrageously expensive brew (a mixture of five coffees individually prepared) and get warm again. One often chooses his coffee house according to the kind of musical recordings played there—Symphony, Jazz, Rock-and-Roll, Baroque Chamber Music, Dixieland, all available. If it is earlier than 10 A. M., a gift of some toast or an egg may accompany the coffee. This is called "Sarvice," and the gracious custom is slowly disappearing from the coffee-houses I frequent.

At one such place, in the busy Gion corner of downtown Kyoto, I meet the new wife of the handsome young brother who delivers for the place by motorcycle (business people generally eat their meals, and between-meal snacks, in their offices). His parents, as well as his brother and *his* wife and children, live together in the tiny space behind the bar. So small is the shop that much ingenuity is used; the water is heated on the "denki," the inevitable electric heater, and the delicious cakes and other delicacies are kept in a glass-covered case outside. Several years later I will return to this place to again see the pretty "new" wife—acquired from the island of Kyushuu by newspaper advertisement—and the handsome baby who has increased the resident population. My friend, the young father, sits at a table with me and strums guitar while he practises his halting English; his wife is hard at work in the kitchen. I was much surprised when another companion sipping coffee, a young University instructor, said: "They are talking to you as though you were the Emperor!"

I hadn't realized the grandparents were using the most polite Japanese to me (there are at least three levels of politeness to choose from in making ordinary conversation, and subtlety in Japanese consists as much in choosing the appropriate level as in selecting the precise expressions to be used). It was always hard to persuade them to let me pay for my refreshments, even when I had a guest to share the cake and milk-coffee (cafe-au-lait). "Stone san is a good-will ambassador!" murmured an Art critic I knew, and I protested. It was so easy to feel at home with these happy, crowded folk. On New Year's Eve, an important time in Japan when the temple bells ring 108 times at midnight, the little shop is always closed to the public and there is a party, for invited guests only (including this lucky visitor). Nearby, a narrow river flows through downtown Kyoto, on the banks of which are tourist traps where Western-style floor shows are performed (terrible, and very expensive, with some nudity). Leading into this thoroughfare are other, narrower streets of much antiquity, where old shops with great Art treasures abound. On New Year's Eve, emerging from this gemuchlicht party, how nice to see these formidable places, some with small tea-house gardens behind the showrooms, shining in the frosty moonlight! Female figures in kimono, and others in mini-skirt, go softly across the busy bridge next to the Kabuki theater. There is something in the air, but, what it is, I cannot say. Earlier, at dinner with a Zen Priest, his wife, and family, there has been a hint of mysteries as we eat from ancient lacquered boxes. After New Year's Eve, during the long Shogatsu New Year's celebration, everything will be closed tight, but on the day and night before New Year's there is great activity, as friends hurry to-and-fro delivering gifts. With the Chinese, this is a great feast time, to recompense for a year of disappointment. How often does the brightly greeted New Year come up to our expectations? We are all one year older, and remorse and self-recrimination often go very deep. In the meantime, we play at the gaiety of New Year's Eve, and this brings us closer to our neighbors. To share an emotion is sweet; to suffer alone can be very bitter.

CHAPTER 3

WABI SABI

To understand Japanese people at all, one must know something of the Wabi Sabi concept. The Japanese sense of beauty, unlike some of the gaudy Chinese manifestations, usually relies on delicate understatement. What is left out is as important as what is put in. A cultivated Japanese man changes the hanging scroll in his Tokonoma about as regularly as he does the flower arrangement in front of it. If he owns a hundred such treasures, he will usually show only one at a time. The idea of displaying all his treasured possessions, as with the New York City entrepreneur who shocked me by having Old Masters hanging all the way up the staircase–and in the bathrooms!–would seem inconceivably vulgar to him. A "one corner" black and white Sumi-e painting will show all the action in a small part of the scroll; the viewer's imagination can vividly take care of the rest. So a stark drawing of what seems to be a man in a small boat, with nothing else, in our sight becomes a graphic portrait of a stormy ocean with the lone fisherman riding out the swells to the promontory of land behind. As with sex, what is suggested is far stronger than that which is explicitly stated. How subtle the pathway, in the traditional Japanese garden, that leads nowhere! A sure commentary on living!

Having mentioned what I consider the acme of Art in the most aesthetic of countries, Japan–I am speaking of the living, changing Japanese Garden–it would seem wise to include here a commentary on the Zen garden as I once found it written in a text. Unfortunately, I do not have the name of the writer, though there is the vague recollection that he was a University Professor. Should this ignorance be rectified, it would be my hope to include his name in a future edition of this book. I do not want the reader to think this profound commentary is mine!

SEVEN PRINCIPLES OF A JAPANESE ZEN GARDEN

(Note: Flowers are never used on the dining table or at odd points about the house, in Japan; never worn as corsages; never used at weddings or funerals. Essentially as a matter of philosophy, flowers are considered to have a very special life of their own and are never used as decoration.)

In summary, the basic philosophy of the Japanese house and garden resolves itself about the seven principles of Zen, which, freely translated, are as follows:

FUKINSEI—Assymmetry or dissymmetry; suggesting things which are irregular. The opposite of geometric circles or squares.

KANSO—Simplicity; without gaudiness, not heavy or gross; clean, neat, and fresh; yet reserved, frank, and truthful; not ornate.

KOKO—Austerity, maturity, reduction to essentials; lack of sensuousness; refers to things that are aged, weathered, venerable.

SHIZEN—Naturalness, artlessness, absence of pretense and artificiality. It does not mean raw nature; it involves full creative intent, but should not be forced; unselfconsciousness; true naturalness that is a negation of the naive and accidental.

YUGEN—Subtly profound; suggestion rather than total revelation; things not wholly revealed but partly hidden from view; shadow and darkness; hence Yugen involves the shadow area of the garden.

DATSUZEKU—Unworldliness; freedom from use of "compasses and rulers," freedom from worldly attachments, bondage, and restrictive laws. It involves transcendence of conventional usage. It is often a surprise element or an astonishing characteristic.

SEIJAKU—Quietness, calmness, and silence; the opposite of disturbance. In the Orient there is a saying that "Stillness is activity." This characteristic should be strongly felt in a Japanese garden.

This is, of course, far more than a description of a Zen garden! It is actually instruction in the Zen way of thinking, and a glimpse of the traditional Japanese restraint so foreign to the West (and disappearing so rapidly in Japan!).

It is said that the four essentials of the Japanese Tea Ceremony (Cha No Yu), as with Zen itself, are: Harmony, Respect, Purity, Serenity. There is an exquisiteness in a black-and-white scroll of a lone bird on a dead branch in winter, or a wild flower growing on a barren rock – a feeling of livingness and a seemingly absurd inner gratitude that no amount of self-canceling lushness could ever afford. Reducing life to such bare essentials, we feel the overwhelming immensity of it all.

To define "Wabi Sabi" seems impossible, even when we know that the "sabi" part is related to the adjective "sabishi," which implies a loneliness. I have often talked to Japanese scholars about the meaning–as with the related noun, shibui–but none have dared define what it really is, though almost all Japanese will agree on any example of Wabi Sabi. For instance, some language students of mine in Japan–failing utterly to *explain* Wabi Sabi–all agreed that the famous gate in the ocean at Miajima was much too red and *not* Wabi Sabi at all. "Perhaps in a hundred years it may become so," explained one embarrassed student, a University graduate. All agreed that the unfinished interior of Ginkakuji (the Silver Pavilion in Kyoto) was Wabi Sabi, and all denied that the much-photographed and ornate Gold Pavilion (Kinkakuji) had any element of Wabi Sabi in it.

"The interior of Ginkakuji is dear to my heart," admitted one slightly inebriated student, who would never have made such a stark statement if he had not been drinking sake and beer for several hours. I understood him to mean that the Wabi Sabi quality of Ginkakuji caused him to feel particularly Japanese, a warm and unsharable feeling.

In an old issue of the "Middle Way," a Buddhist publication from England, I accidentally came upon a passage by my old friend, Zen Priest Sohaku Ogata (now deceased) that seems to aptly illustrate Wabi Sabi. I quote in part:

> "Sen-no-Rikyu is considered the father of the Tea-cult. One summer he grew morning glories in his garden, and their loveliness became known among his friends. Toyotomi Hideyoshi, the generalissimo, heard of the beauty of these flowers and wanted to see them. Rikyu, learning

> of this, invited Hideyoshi to a tea party in his retreat.
>
> When the generalissimo (who was the Tea Master's sponsor) entered Rikyu's garden, to his surprise there were no morning glories at all. They had been cut down, and not a flower was to be seen. Dismayed, he said nothing; but when he entered the teahouse, there in front of him was one spray in a bamboo vase—the essence of Morning Glory. Hideyoshi, the distinguished guest, was immensely pleased. He was able, in a setting of utter simplicity and cleanliness, to experience fully the unique beauty of the flower.

And then Ogata sensei goes on to tell a second story:

> One morning after a stormy night, Kago-no-Chiyo, a famous Haiku poetess, went to her well to draw water. She found a vine of morning glory, bearing a beautiful flower, which had blown down and entwined itself around the handle of the water-bucket.
>
> Such fragile beauty should not be disturbed, she said to herself, to accommodate such a practical need as drawing water. As she went to a neighbor to borrow some, instead, her nature-loving impulse asserted itself and her poetic genius woke up. She wrote:
>
> Being captured, my well bucket,
> I beg for water from my neighbor.

The "fuller, more complete" approach to life and feeling suggested in Kago-no-Chiyo's actions, the willingness to accept and affirm life more purely, with naturalness and directness, in each moment as it is found, without conditioned intellect and response, represents the Wabi or Sabi life." As well as Zen.

Such stories absolutely knock me out. I must admit they might not be everybody's cup of tea, however. Being in Japan during the 1964 Olympics there, I remember the Japanese people's well-concealed chagrin when the Russian athletes, being asked to take part in a Tea Ceremony, simply snorted, "All that fuss for a cup of tea!"

One time, in Los Angeles, an old painter friend and I went, together, to see a Japanese exhibit at the Art Museum. Afterwards, we idly wandered into the Italian section of the Museum. My sensitive friend took one look and shuddered. Coming immediately after the delicate statement of the Japanese scrolls, the lush and opulent colors of the great Italian work were too much of a jolt to the system. Both have their place, but not together! There is much of aesthetic—and philosophic—value to be derived from this understated, austere, pseudo-natural approach of the Japanese. Many times, when we admire a Tea-house or the rock formations of a garden, we are startled to realize that the work is not natural at all, not an imitation of nature. It had used the natural as a starting point and gone on to develop a Wabi Sabi aesthetic from there. So nature became a point of departure. As my friend, Masao Abe, the eminent Buddhist scholar, declared: "Fukinsei—certainly a Wabi Sabi characteristic—does not mean 'assymetrical' at all. Rather, it implies going *beyond* symmetry." This reminds me of the Jazz instrumentalist who must learn technique so he can forget technique in freeing himself to express what cannot really be expressed.

To find the greatest beauty in a weathered old door—or person—implies respect for that which has lived and endured. Such respect for age is endemic in the Oriental way of thought. And haven't we all felt an admiration for the features of an old woman who has had children and grandchildren and known triumphs and times of despair? Can any paint do to wood what the harsh hands of Time will do? One of my favorite buildings is a small Art Gallery near Big Sur, California, built from the discarded timbers of an old bridge. This wood has never been painted; it is indelibly stained by time. A new car has little character, but, when we see an ancient "Classic," we involuntarily gasp with admiration. Old manuscripts and examples of calligraphy that have been burned in fires are greatly prized in Japan. I, myself, find moss-covered stones that take the place of pavement in many areas highly evocative of the past and pleasing to the Spirit. The rapidly changing old Capital of Kyoto has always afforded me an aesthetic bath. Even more is this Wabi Sabi felt in the mountains, where one spies a heavy iron kettle hanging by bamboo from the ceiling, over an open hole in the floor, made to hold charcoal. What a wonderful way to boil water for tea and cook the vegetables so important in the country way of eating!

The Mysterious 108

The number 108 holds within it a great mystery, but I have never found anyone who could explain this mystery to me.

Of course, there are 108 beads in both the Hindu and the Buddhist rosaries.

There are 108 movements in T'ai Chi Ch'uan.

In Kyoto, and other ancient places in Japan, the temple bells ring 108 times at Midnight on New Year's Eve.

In ancient China, the malefactor usually received 108 blows as punishment.

In India, there are 108 principal Upanishads.

The great river, Ganges, is said to have 108 names.

108 maids are supposed to have danced simultaneously with Krishna in his great Rasa dance.

It is believed that Holy Men know 108 names of the God, Vishnu.

In the Scriptures of India there are 9 steps to the 12 Nidanas–making a total of 108.

In Buddhism there are 36 Klesas (Afflictions)–in the past, present, and future. 3 times 36 is 108.

There are said to be 108 Mudras (hand positions).

Shiva gave 108 instructions to his Consort, Devi, in the Tantras.

108 Brahmins were summoned to Buddha's birth to foretell his destiny (according to Myth).

The Burmese "Footprints of Buddha" are said to have 108 sub-divisions.

The Tibetan Sacred writings called KAHGYUR have 108 volumes.

The White Pagoda in Peking has 108 columns.

It is said that BRAHMA lives for 108 BRAHMA years.

In India, it used to be customary to give 108 rupees as alms.

One day I hope to find the meaning behind this number, 108. There are so many other instances of the number coming into play–not 107, not 109, but always 108. Often Indian Gurus will say: "You are 108,000 miles from the Truth!" (Ramana Maharshi used this expression). Why 108?

Thanks, Robert, for the help in assembling these facts.

CHAPTER 4

CHINESE TAOISTS

There is a profound difference between the life-negating pessimism of traditional Indian Buddhism and the life-prolonging immortality-seeking attitude of Chinese Taoists.

The Indian Buddhist sees the world as a place of complete impermanence, a forest ablaze with suffering. The only answer is to escape from the forest, and this must be done by renouncing individualized existence (for the "Bliss" of Nirvana). "Getting off the wheel of Life and Death" is the goal of all traditional Indian religious philosophy. This complete Idealism of the Buddha's was conscurred in by the sages Vasistha and Ramana Maharshi, though the latter two used different language than the Compassionate One, and, indeed, by all Advaitic (Non-Dual) thought in India, where the aim has always been to find Release, or Salvation, through merging in that greater than ourselves. "Individualized Life is the sin," points out the Maharshi, "and, as such, can only lead to untold suffering." This is compatible with the Buddha's idea of An-Atman, meaning No Entity, No Soul, No Individual Life at all in the final analysis.

Taoism—and Taoist-influenced Zen—feels, on the other hand, that we find our Nirvana right in the midst of the tears and woe, and that Samsara (this world of suffering) *is,* itself, Nirvana when seen properly. The Taoist so enjoys his life that he has always felt one should try for immortality-in-the-body, the much-misunderstood Taoist Alchemy. Longevity, pointing to a love of life ("clinging to life" from the Indian Buddhist point of view), has always been the ideal of the Chinese, who enjoy their food, their sex, and their communal existence, in contrast to the solitude-seeking Indian Holy men, the Gurus and the Disciples.

How can we reconcile these two opposing views of the same existence?

I once knew two women who looked a great deal alike and were so often mistaken for one another. One was attractive and well-groomed , the other was dowdy and rather haggish. Despite these differences, there was no doubt of the startling resemblance.

Again, when there is an accident at an intersection, twelve people view it. Coming into court, each will give a different account of what has happened, despite the fact that they are all speaking of the same accident.

There is only one mountain, but, to the surveyor, it appears in different sections. So, too, the one existence appears in innumerable ways to us, depending on where each of us stands. The world, truly, is a subjective experience, not an object to be perceived the same by all.

Similarly, each of the religious viewpoints is right from its own point of reference. Perhaps the Buddha was speaking of Ultimates, while others were seeking to find workable formulas, including the ones that would send us to Heaven rather than its opposite number.

Still, it is difficult for a sincere seeker to reconcile the opposing viewpoints. From the Indian Sage's corner, the world is not real as there is nothing lasting in it, nothing that is not changing in every second. Nothing has its own continuing identity, but is in a constant state of becoming. So the Upanishads speak of Moksha (Release) from the incessant rounds of suffering in meaningless life after life. The Buddha points the way to the Cessation of Suffering by urging us to merge into the undifferentiated whole. The simpler Indian doctrines speak of devotion to a God and repetition of His Name, which will lead to a Heaven or the Brahma world.

These are in sharp contrast to the Chinese and Japanese outlook, which feels that this life is decidedly worthwhile and prolongation of it is desirous. In such wordly clinging (as opposed to other-world thinking) there is little thought of a next life on earth. Traditionally, death of a Japanese entitles him or her to become a Kami (a minor god or spirit), after which he will stay close to his Clan, in a disembodied condition, helping to prevent disasters to his people. This is part of the "Ancestor Worship" of the Japanese, and it often carries over into Japanese Buddhism and other foreign beliefs.

So, whom are we to believe? It is understandable how the hot, dried-out sub-continent of India, with its continual starvation, would lead to pessimistic views. Yet, China, too, has always had great poverty and starvation, and the Chinese character molded in a colder climate has always stood for great vitality and love of life. The whole world enjoys Chinese food; the great Sage, Confucius, was a practical man who instructed on how to live in human society. He spoke not at all of future lives.

Now, of course, would be the time for the writer to step forward and offer a pat solution, a workable philosophy welding together the different points of view. Such is not possible. To enjoy the sunset and the beauties of Nature is not hard, yet the Yogi, and the Buddha's original followers, say we must ignore the sensory, which represents only ignorance. Because it is pleasing to the taste and the eyes does not make it good or useful. The Upanishads warn us that man mistakes the Pleasing for the Good (meaning Good in the constructive, not the moral, sense). Seeking enjoyment, will we find only suffering?

Probably, for the little-evolved average person, a middle way is best. "Each according to his need" might be my answer, and by "need" we don't mean "desire." Our needs are few, our uncontrolled desires endless. If there is a "need" for Ultimate answers, one must follow a way leading to Ultimates, such as the Buddha's Way. This entails endless sacrifice, the "fasting" implied in Chuang-Tzu's "Fasting Mind." We must drop the non-constructive, no matter how inviting, to reach the Ultimate known as Kensho (complete Enlightenment) in Japanese.

On the other hand, if we are not introspective and not even aware that there might be Ultimate Answers, how can we go down a road that requires some degree of asceticism? The mind untrained in Concentration cannot be expected to stick, single-mindedly, to a formula of life that denies us so much of what we usually want. Family, career, all pursuit of such worldly activities, can only block the way to Ultimate Answers. And yet, we can't all be Monks or recluses, either in or out of the world.

To live each day with some contemplation, and to try to feel gratitude for the really countless blessings we take for granted, will lead us to treat others as we, ourselves, wish to be treated. Simple though these two activities may sound, the effects are profound. Will the average person offer "thanks" when the help is late, or the Stock Market down? Will he take time from a busy schedule to go within and explore the giant world of inner space? Not very many will do those two things. And yet, each of us perceives his own self-caused suffering! Why is one unwilling to give up his crutches and the very habits responsible for this suffering? We cling to what hurts us most. And all clinging, of whatever nature, ultimately leads to unhappiness. "Hang loose" is preferable to "Hang in there, baby," we must conclude.

CHAPTER 5

THE SILENT SADHU

The lengthening twilight seemed almost interminable as the old car plowed along the dismal roads east of Baroda. Indian sunsets are particularly spectacular where there is flat country and few trees or buildings to break the magnificent vista of pink, orange, and purple sky. These roads had not been built for motor vehicles, and our progress was slow as we pushed past numerous workers hurrying home on their bicycles. I had been warned the journey might take more than two hours.

Inside the old Ambassador, the only car the government of India allowed to be built, there were the three self-styled "Young Turks" and myself, the somewhat mysterious visitor from the West staying with a Patel family on Race Course Road. The "Young Turks," all University graduate students, thought of themselves as rebels against traditional Indian life. I remembered that, when the distinguished scholar and President of India, Radhakrishnan, had come to Baroda to give a talk, the "Young Turks" and their friends had boycotted the occasion, though everybody who was anybody in the ancient city made sure to be present for the distinguished man's speech.

Now they were taking me to meet a famous Sadhu, a traditional Holy Man, living not too far from Baroda. Contrary to popular belief in the West, Holy Men are not common in India these days, particularly in the busy business cities. If one wants to meet Saints, he must go to Varanasi (Benares) or up north to Rishakesh and Almora--and not all the "Saints" he sees will be genuine. So the "Young Turks" were, somewhat cynically, taking their new western friend to meet a reputed Sage.

The journey finally ended, just as darkness descended, in a desolate field with one strange building standing some distance from the road. Looking like a huge house, it had no glass where the windows should have been (one often finds birds flying in the house in

India) and, in some parts, no roof over the wooden floor. Entering, we found a variegated scene. One man was cooking a banana over a fire smoldering on the floor, several others were reading musty manuscripts that looked a thousand years old, several were sitting cross-legged in attitudes of meditation, and others were milling around, talking. The main light was from the fire, though one or two candles also burned. One had the feeling of being half-inside and half-outside in that house. Incomprehensibly, a well-milked goat roamed freely about the rooms.

We were told the Sadhu had been in Samadhi (super-conscious state) since the day before, and there was no telling when he might emerge from his exalted condition. We decided to wait.

Most of the conversation seemed to be in Gujarati, the language of the local province, but a few of those present spoke English (the University language in India) as well. It was hard to tell what the others were doing there. Did some live in that huge house? Were they disciples of the Sadhu? It was impossible to know.

After about an hour, there was a sudden silence. Looking up, we saw a strange, almost drunken-looking man entering through a doorway, leaning lightly against the wall. He had on a simple white dhoti instead of the ochre-colored Sanyasi robe we half-expected.

This imposing man, of indeterminate age (was he 40? 50? 60? The white beard made it hard to tell) was now the focus of all eyes. He quietly sat down in the cross-legged Lotus posture, not saying a word. There was silence for quite a while. Then, one-by-one, overcome by the august presence of the man, the young Turks came forward, prostrated themselves on the floor, and kissed his bare feet in the traditional Indian gesture of respect. So much for their cynicism!

Finally, it was my turn, and I carefully seated myself in meditation pose about two feet from the Sadhu, facing him. We looked at each other, but no word was spoken (I had no way of even knowing if he understood English).

After a while, one of the young Turks came forward and whispered in my ear: "Ask him something!"

I paid no attention. Sitting so close to the man, who had just emerged from the deepest of immersions, I was fascinated by the tremendous vibration of livingness about him. Outwardly, he moved not at all, but inwardly he must have been seething with a tremendous force flowing through him; the tight clasp of the hands, with only the fingers moving, gave some clue to the dynamic surge inside. He had come out of Samadhi, evidently sensing visitors were there to see him, and yet he was still in it. Those who have successfully practised really deep meditation will have some inkling of what was surging inside him, but there is no way to name it.

How long we sat, I cannot recall. I had been drawn into his radius of one-pointed dynamism, and words would have been superfluous. Again and again one of the "Young Turks" would come up to me and whisper: "Ask him something!" Evidently they felt I would pose a significant question or two, he would give the answers, and the Secret of the Universe would be clearly revealed. How naive can we be to believe such things are contained in words!

Except for the writhing of the fingers, clasped tight as though to keep him from exploding, the Sadhu didn't move, and he never said a word during the hours of our visit. After his first sharp glance at me, he never again looked up, his half-closed eyes remaining unseeingly focused on the floor between us. The electricity in our little circle never wavered, actually seeming to grow in intensity all the time we sat there.

Finally, I felt it was time to go; we had intruded enough. Standing, I made the hand gesture known as Pronam to the Holy Man, who did not return it; instead, he gave me another sharp, but not unfriendly, look. Turning quickly, I led the way from the room, past the fire (where several men were now cooking some greens), past the over-milked goat, and out into the deep darkness lighted by a million stars above. We each took several deep breaths of the still-warm evening air and then got into the car parked by the side of the house.

The drive back was swift and quiet. I was still under the spell of the Sadhu, and the others were rather taken back by, and ashamed of, their impulsive act of respect to the Holy Man.

One time, on the long drive, one of the young men (the son of a Baroda Doctor) asked me why I hadn't questioned the

Sadhu so as to get some answers.

I smiled for a moment. "Do you mean to tell me you missed the whole thing?" I demanded.

He was surprised. What "whole thing" had he missed? What had happened? But I was not of a mind to speak anymore, and we rode the rest of the way in silence. I was filled with the vibrance of the Sadhu, who had been so deep in his God-intoxicated state. I do not know what thoughts or feelings occupied the others.

CHAPTER 6

PYRAMID POETRY

Haiku, the Japanese 17-syllable poems, have become exceedingly popular in the West. Many translations, some in rhyme and some not, have appeared of the works of Basho, Buson, Issa, and others. Frequently, Westerners have attempted to write in the familiar three-line (5 syllable, 7 syllable, 5 syllable) manner, but they have discovered that Haiku does not lend itself readily to original works in English. The Japanese language has a different construction from that of English (traditionally, the Japanese "syllables" called Hirogana, not the Chinese writing known as Kanji, are used in Haiku). So English 17-syllable poems usually appear stilted and without impact.

To meet this difficulty, I have invented a form I call "Pyramid Poetry" (actually, the shape of the poem is like that of a diamond). The first line has one syllable, the second two syllables, the third three, and the fourth four. Then the fifth line has three again, the sixth only two, and the seventh and last line has only one syllable, which should, ideally, be explosive, or at least put a powerful climax to the whole poem.

Thus the construction looks like this:

—
— —
— — —
— — — —
— — —
— —
—

An example might be the following:

THE
STIF–LING
HEAT IS GONE–
HOW WEL–COME IS
THE SUD–DEN
SUM–MER
SHOW'R!

Another, perhaps stronger, poem, with a powerful last syllable, is:

TRY
TO PRAY
KEEP–ING NAUGHT
BUT THOUGHTS OF GOD
AND NO MORE
THOUGHT OF
YOU!

These are fun to make, and seem to be relatively easy in either English or Japanese. At times students and I have spent an entire evening composing,and reading aloud, these Pyramid Poems. I recommend this activity very highly. Turn off the deadly Television set and come to life; offer a little creativity. We have gotten so used to spectator sports and television dramas that actual participation may require a particular effort. No matter! Let some experience come to the surface and try to express it in this one, two, three, four, three, two, one syllable form. You may surprise yourself!

OH
REST–LESS
SAF–FRON MONK;
JUST WHAT DO YOU
HOPE TO GAIN?
YOU MUST
DIE!

HOW
CAN WE
HOPE TO BUILD
A BET–TER WORLD
UN–LESS WE
CHANGE OUR
SELVES?

CHAPTER 7

THE GRAND PLAN & THE I CHING

Events continually happen to me as though there is some Grand Plan being carried out. No matter how I try, I cannot seem to go against the form of this plan. If one can flow easily with the current, all goes well—but it, seemingly, will reach the predetermined end, no matter what.

When I leave a place, with nothing certain about the future, I know the events to come are already formed, but not yet visible, as the future sculpture lies within the untouched marble cube. So, secure in faith, one can wait patiently and the inevitable will arrive. Several examples are the following:

Not having gone to Japan from San Francisco, as planned, I found myself in New Mexico, instead. I decided to take an apartment in Santa Fe and build my future there, but two visits did not turn up a place to stay. Resting in Taos, at a friend's house, I awoke one rainy Monday morning with the feeling that I should be in Albuquerque, a place concerning which I had never evinced the slightest interest. So anxious was I to get there (for no apparent reason) that I did not wait to collect my laundry, but asked my host to pick it up and forward it to me. Then I took off on the 130-mile drive, in the rain, to the larger city.

Arriving in Albuquerque, I did not even know which Freeway exit to take. Finding one, I emerged on a main street and parked in front of a bookstore. Inside, I asked some unimportant question. The man behind the counter idly inquired what sort of work I did, and I gave the first answer that came into my head: "I guess I teach T'ai Chi Ch'uan."

Immediately two students jumped up from behind the books and said: "We've been waiting a long time for a T'ai Chi teacher to arrive!"

I protested that I was not in Albuquerque to stay, had no

place to live, no studio in which to teach, etc. All the answers were forthcoming, however. Within three days, six weekly classes had been organized at a nearby Yoga Academy. From this "accidental" beginning came three full years of teaching Oriental subjects at the two Universities, of teaching English language to young business men from Japan, even of designing a series of Zen cards and note paper! The books and other matters followed, all as though pre-arranged—all, seemingly, because of an urge to go to a strange city and a careless answer to a question.

— — —

My first trip to Japan took place because a new-found friend, a Dr. C- - -, suggested I accompany her to Kyoto (where she had lived before) and take a job teaching English at Kyoto University. It wasn't until just before the boat was to leave that I found out (1) the teaching job was fiction, and (2) she was not going to Japan as planned. I took the freighter, anyway, the only passenger on the boat (which turned out to be carrying dangerous explosives).

Expecting to arrive in Yokahama (the port for Tokyo), we turned up in Kobe, instead. Somehow, I made my way to Kyoto, and was delighted to find that I would be able to stay in a Zen temple after one week. I determined to use that week to travel to Tokyo and try to find my friend Reps, who was then living in Japan.

At that time there was no super-express train between cities. My car on the old-style train was half-empty, and I decided to spend the five or six hours of the trip practising my limited Japanese with home-made flash cards.

A fine-looking Japanese man entered the car soon after I sat down. He hesitated a moment, trying to decide which empty seat to take. Then, on impulse, he sat down next to me; later, he told me the flash-cards had interested and amused him.

This was one of the most significant meetings of my life. In future years I was to often stay at the Tenrikyo Church community, in Kyoto, where Reverend Takahashi, my new acquaintance, was a minister. Today we call each other "kyodai," meaning "brother." Perhaps I have had some small influence in bringing their church to this country. Largely because of their kindness and hospitality, I think of Kyoto, today, as my home as much as any place in the world. All because of some crude flash-cards with Japanese characters on them!

— — —

After a long, dusty train-ride from Bombay (ten tickets had been sold for the six places in our compartment!) I arrived in Baroda in central India. It was not easy to find the Vishva Jyoti Ashram, to which Swami Krishnanand had invited me when he was in America, as it was deep in the countryside. Arriving there, I was dismayed to find that Swamiji had left (for many years, it turned out) the day before!

What to do? I returned to the Baroda station, and began to walk aimlessly around town. Few seemed to speak English, and I wondered what I would do when darkness descended. Idly, I noticed two young men playing badminton. Thinking they might be University students, who would speak English, I walked over to the game and addressed myself to one of the players.

"Do you play chess?" he asked irrelevantly, ignoring my question.

"Sure, I play chess. Why?" was my puzzled answer.

" Come live with us and play chess with my father and myself!" exhorted my new friend, Kaushik. By evening I was installed in their part of a two-family house, where only the father, a fine, religious man, spoke English besides Kaushik, the oldest son. The two younger sons (one with a wracking cough) slept in a room with the father, who read a scripture to them each night before bed. The mother stayed behind the kitchen with the servant. Sorrowfully, I could not communicate with them at all during my stay, even to ask them to make the curry and red tea less pungent, if possible (it was hot!).

Never did I win a chess game from the expert Kaushik (who had often played simultaneous games against ten or twelve students), except for the one day he was greatly upset. That day, surprised at the first obvious blunder I had ever seen him make, I asked him what was wrong.

"The marriage is off!" he blurted out; there were tears in his eyes.

His parents had arranged a suitable marriage with a girl from Bombay, which was to take place shortly after I left Baroda. The Caste was right, the Astrology signs checked out, and everything seemed appropriate and auspicious. He had even been allowed to meet the girl, whom he liked.

"Why, Kaushik?" I exclaimed, in astonishment.

"In our Caste, the cousins arrange the preliminaries," he explained. "It is our custom to make gifts to each other of some gold, a Sari, and some chocolate. The other people did not give all they should have, and my cousins were offended, so they called off the wedding!"

"Nonsense!" I countered. "How do you know *your* cousins didn't fudge on *your* gifts? You take the first train to Bombay, see this lovely girl, and tell her you want to marry her!"

Kaushik shook his head, mournfully. "Things aren't done that way here. I'll never see her again," he predicted. And, illogically, that is exactly how it turned out. After that day I never won another chess game from Kaushik, in whose home I had such a lovely stay. Looking back, because he did not choose to answer a question of mine, I was able, for the first time, to get a close-up view of Indian family life, for which I was very grateful.

— — —

All this is preliminary to the story I really want to tell, however. It involves the I CHING, the ancient BOOK OF CHANGES that has played such an important role in the building of Chinese culture.

The ship on which I was traveling had put into Hong Kong harbor for repairs, and we were tied up at Kowloon for quite a few days. This gave my new friend, Mr. Liu (whom I had met through a letter from Reps) a chance to show me his fine Art Gallery, to do an amazing reading of the lines on my hand, and to arrange a dinner with some old Buddhas who crossed over from Red China (Mr. Liu was a fine, and knowledgeable, Taoist). By the time the boat was repaired and we were underway, I was much indebted to the kind Mr. Liu.

Our dinner took place at an old restaurant near the Art Gallery on Cameron Road. We did not eat downstairs with the other diners, however, but had a special table upstairs, from where we could get a good view of the gambling room behind open curtains. I had no idea if the gambling was legal, but there was certainly a lot of action going on. Being well aware of the Chinese propensity for gambling of all types (rich Chinese who live on the English side of Hong Kong, though unable to speak English, open the day-old Wall Street Journal to the Stock Market page every day and are remarkably well-informed on what is transpiring in Wall Street), I was not surprised to see several young mothers standing, and, apparently, playing, with infants in their arms. I had no idea what kind of gambling was taking place, but the pace was rather feverish. When our party was seated, we began to drink quite a lot of warm Chinese rice-wine, which is very mellowing. It soon became apparent that Mr. Liu and his erudite friend, Mr. Tung, were the only ones, besides myself, who spoke English, but this didn't seem to hamper the conversation, which was on an increasingly deep level, mostly about Taoist concepts. Soon a steady procession of tasty dishes—such as almonds cooked in a rich sauce—found their way to the center of our table, from where we speared them with our chopsticks in the Chinese fashion. No dish was on the table more than a few minutes; just long enough for a taste, and then it was gone, to be replaced by another in the seemingly endless stream of delicacies.

I remember thinking: "These 'ascetics' really eat well!" There was a pleasant haze from the wine, a feeling of well-being from the delicious food, and a heightened sense of awareness as we leisurely explored the Cosmos together. I remembered what another Chinese host had once said to me: "You have come a long way. The least we can do is offer you good food and good company." Remarkably civilized people, the Chinese!

When the evening regretfully ended, my new acquaintance, Mr. Tung, took me aside and said he had something to give me the following day before my boat left. I was surprised, but arranged to have tea with him on the balcony in the giant terminal next to our ship's berth.

The next day Mr. Tung arrived exactly on time, carrying a slim red book under his arm. He handed it to me with a triumphant smile.

"Thank you," I said somewhat hesitantly. A quick glimpse had revealed that the book was written entirely in Chinese, which I do not read.

"This book contains a mathematical discussion of the I CHING," he explained, the latter, of course, being the Chinese "Book of Changes," which can be used for Divination, as a work of deepest philosophy, or as a source from which to study three thousand years of Chinese Culture.

"I want you to take it with you," he continued in a kindly manner. "You will have need of it."

"But I don't read Chinese," I protested. "And I have such limited space! Traveling across the world for a year, staying in snowy countries, in jungles, and in big cities, I have had to throw out everything extraneous so I can get by with just one bag. Forgive me for seeming ungrateful, but - - -"

He shook his head decisively. "Take the book!" he commanded. "You will see!" With that he handed it to me, rose, and was gone in an instant, through the dense crowd packing the terminal.

I stared at the book, which seemed useless to me. Nevertheless, it was not large and had many fascinating diagrams, which I thought I might examine at another time. So I placed it in a pocket of my carry-all bag and promptly forgot all about it. This was probably in November.

Almost a year later, in Autumn, I returned to Los Angeles by plane from New York, having completed my swing to the West through India, Africa, etc. One of the first people I phoned upon my arrival in Los Angeles was my good friend, the eminent scholar, Professor Huang.

"I am glad you arrived back today!" he exclaimed in a delighted tone of voice. "This afternoon I am giving a talk, to a large audience, on the I CHING, and I would like you to come with me to hear it."

Something clicked in my mind, something I had forgotten for so many months. Asking the Professor to wait a moment, I went to my unpacked bag. Sure enough, the slim red volume was still there.

"Professor Huang," I spoke into the phone. "I have a book about the I CHING, which I have been carrying around the world for almost a year. Would you like to see it?"

I could visualize his indulgent smile at the other end. "Thank you, but I think I am familiar with all the I CHING commentaries. The only book I would be interested in is a rare volume of mathematical calculations on the I CHING, which I once saw, many, many years ago in Shanghai. But that book was written in Chinese!"

I hastily explained that this book, too, was in Chinese and contained a mathematical system of the I CHING. I begged Professor Huang not to move, that I would be right over as quickly as traffic would allow.

When I arrived, Professor Huang took one look at the book and stated: "I have waited thirty years to find this volume!" He then opened to the first page, on which Mr. Tung had evidently written a fitting inscription, seemingly aware that the book would find its way into the Professor's hands.

A broad smile was on the older man's face as he read the long inscription, written carefully in beautiful Chinese characters. He did not attempt to interpret the message for me, but it was obvious that Mr. Tung's message had hit its mark. Seldom have I seen the Professor smile so brightly. Then, placing the book under his arm, he walked briskly to the car with me, and soon we were on our way to his lecture. I have often wondered, through the years, whether Mr. Tung might not have been the author of the mysterious book.

Prayer For Buddhists (and others) Before Meals

May I be properly grateful for this food,

which is the result of the work of others, and the suffering of other forms of life.

May I always be grateful to the Buddha,

Who was born at Kapilavastu,

Enlightened at Magadha,

Preached at Varanasi,

And died at Kushinagara.

I now open the Tathagata's* eating bowl for my meal.

May I, and all others,

Be delivered from self-clinging.

May we be led from the unreal to the real,

From darkness into light,

Bringing an end to the suffering of all beings.

*Tathagata–Another name for the Buddha, meaning "the One Who thus comes."

CHAPTER 8

OU MIE SHU

There is a quality about OU MIE SHU'S drawings – and the captions with which he inscribes them–that I can only describe as Simple Humanity. Not only is he a skilled craftsman in his drawing, but it seems obvious that he is also a poet, despite any English language barrier (I happen to know that he is also a fine cook). Because his work so represents the quality we would like to have in this book, we have arranged with him to include these drawings, which I hope the reader will enjoy as much as I do.

OU MIE SHU now lives in Albuquerque, New Mexico, where he paints, teaches at the Universities, and plays piano and violin for recreation. Consequently, he has many friends in that city, and it is my feeling that he may now make many more with these drawings.

NOTHING IS
EVERYTHING.
NOTHING IS
WITHOUT ANYTHING
NOTHING CAN BE
NOTHING
YET
ANYTHING CAN BE
SOMETHING.

WITHOUT SOUND
THAT IS . . .
WITHOUT FORM
THAT IS . . . .
WITHOUT WORD
THAT IS . . .
WITHOUT LOVE
THAT IS . . . .
WITHOUT . . . WHERE WITHOUT?
IN LIFE . . . ALL WITHIN

OU
MIE
SHU
1968

"MY DEAR FRIEND, REMEMBER OR NOT . . . . .
FORGET US NOT . . . ."

No dream

No nightmare

No joy

No sorrow

. . . .

Just to

warm

my hands

. . . .

Ou Mie Shu

(In Taiwan

Elder people warm hands

with a pot of charcoal in a basket)

一九五七.

TWO
HEARTS
BEAT
TOGETHER

MANY
YEARS
APART.

VERY HAPPY
. . . . .
WE ARE.

OU MIE SHU
1/2 OF
TAIWAN IN 1957

WOMAN FARMER
IN THE FIELD—

I EAT
LIKE A MAN
WORK LIKE
A MAN.
LOOK LIKE
A MAN....
YET..
I AM SHY.

BIG SISTER
HAS NO FATHER
LITTLE SISTER
HAS NO MOTHER
BOTH HAVE EACH OTHER

SOMEDAY.
THEY WILL MEET
MEN WHO HAS
NO FATHER, MOTHER
BROTHER OR SISTER.

OH,
MAN...
ARE
WE
STRANGERS
OR
NO
STRANGERS

OUMIE SHU
1968.

MOURNING
WEARS IN
FUNERALS.
↓
NOT EVERY
MAN IN
MY FAMILY
KNOWS ME.
BUT I
SHARE
THEIR SORROW

ONE BIKE
TEN WOODEN BUCKETS
THIRTY MINUTES RIDE
please........
NO FLAT TIRE..
OR ELSE
BUCKETS WILL
BREAK INTO
PEICES

THEN.....
PEOPLE WILL
LOOK, WILL LAUGH....
MY WIFE WILL CRY.

1957 ME SHU OF SMALL MERCHANTS IN TAIWAN.
RE-WRITTEN AND DRAWN IN OCT 1968 ———

WITHOUT TIME,
THAT IS
WITHOUT SOUND,
THAT IS
WITHOUT WORD,
THAT IS
WITHOUT LOVE,
THAT IS
WHAT IS WITHOUT?

IN LIFE,
WE SHOULD BE
ALL WITHIN.

OF 虎子
TIGER
BOY.

DOGGIE DOG WHAT
people SAY
DOG AS I WHO
sleeps HE MAY . . . . .

SNOW IS FOR YOU

TO SEE,

NOT TO HOLD,

IT COMES

AND IT GOES.

DEAR Justin: It is good to get a card from you, I think, if one can find a few souls that understand and also relate, that is precious, Karate, Kung Fu, Tai Chi or not, it is all God's doing, if men still see God in men, it is pathetic that many cannot even afford to see clear in men being abused and let abused by the pressure and tensions in life's waste. Please take care and do and teach good Tai Chi.

Your friend Mie Shu

CHAPTER 9

THE MEANING OF SUFFERING

The Buddha, 2500 years ago, pointed out that three conditions are common to all beings: Impermanence, Lack of any permanent ego-self, and Suffering. Dukkha, Suffering, means more than pain as the opposite of pleasure, and the Buddha said that such suffering is the inevitable result of Greed, Anger, and Delusion (by delusion is meant mistaking the unreal for the Real).

It is my intention to one day write a book on "The Causes of Suffering," examining these causes on both the existential every-day psychological level and from the deeper, more meaningful Spiritual basis. There is no other single subject so applicable to men, for who has not suffered?

Visiting in Palo Alto, California, I received a phone call from my friends at the Japanese America West (Tenrikyo) church in nearby San Francisco. They had a new automobile, but nobody to drive it. Would I be kind enough to play chauffeur for one day so a group of Ministers and Church members could go to Sacramento for a special ceremony, hear two important sermons by visitors from the main Church in Japan, and return the same night to San Francisco?

I was delighted to be of some help, and, after spending Saturday night at the Church in San Francisco, called for some old people Sunday morning and headed East in the new car.

The two sermons lasted four and one-half hours! It is impossible to concentrate in a foreign language for that long, so, halfway through the afternoon, I borrowed paper and scribbled some thoughts on the Human Condition and the Meaning of Suffering. These had been very strong in my mind because of the plight of people I had just left on the Monterey peninsula, and because of the predicament of the family I was visiting in Palo Alto.

These notes formed themselves into two essays, one on the Human Condition (Suffering), and the other, more hopeful, speaking of the Joy that awaits man if he wants it. The two follow, just as I scribbled them that Sunday afternoon while listening to the talks in Japanese.

The Human Condition

The undisciplined mind can only lead to misery. When we are guided by our desires, and when we play the game within the pleasure-pain syndrome–seeking one and avoiding the other–the resultant suffering is inevitable. The great tragedy comes if we do not learn from the experience, but lead joyless life after life without discernible meaning. To want what we cannot have, to ask that we sustain what is unsustainable, and to demand that the law of continuous change be somehow annulled is to invite unhappiness. Not to look within and introspect what has caused the misery is tantamount to suicide.

Of course, there is a type of natural mind that has almost disappeared from our busy world. One rainy day, in Northern India, I had persuaded a Sikh taxi driver to drive me from New Delhi to the famous town of Hardwar. As we drove through the lightly falling rain, in deepest country, we passed some stacks of hay (or some such growth) piled beside the thin highway. On top of one of these a beautiful boy of about twelve, almost naked, danced as the rain beat down on his head. It was like watching Krishna come to life. Ecstatic in the movements, elbows bent this way and that, he shouted with joy as he moved in response to some Universal guidance. It was a sight I will never forget, like Shiva and Shakti dancing the great cosmic joyous overflowing, the play (Lila) of the Lord. Such an uncluttered, joyous mind is sometimes found among primitives, and also among the Whirling Dervishes, but is rare in our cramped society.

When we pursue status or look for pleasurable time-killers, endless diversion, we find we have empty lives with hollow hearts. On the outside we make pretense to impress others, and inside we feel disturbed and robbed of our just fruits. If we do not belong to an oppressed minority, and if we have enough means to remain solvent, we place our identity in our house or apartment, our car and our children (both possessions), and try to live without an inner ethic or something greater than ourselves. It can't be done successfully, though we can aimlessly divert ourselves if we have the means (I have known wealthy men who amused themselves endlessly with prostitutes and gambling, shutting out any need for looking within. Their family relationships were never very good, however).

We have a duty to find meaning in this very life, this present existential situation, and this requires a disciplined mind. Discontent can be a good starting point if we are willing to recognize it and accept the responsibility for our own lives, both past and future. Discontent and doubt are the first catalysts leading to enlightenment.

In Western Culture, this great ennui and discontent manifests in our forties and our fifties. Long since having abandoned youthful ideals, we feel unfulfilled and bored with ourselves, we transfer the blame to our mates. Rupture of the family serves no purpose—often leads to suicide—unless we are willing to become true "home-leavers" and give up both our desires and our habits. To remake habitual patterns of thought is terribly painful and usually, by the age of forty or fifty, we have lost the ability to pursue change. We rest in the comfortable, and what is comfortable is the habitual that has led to our present condition. "I want to change things!" we say, but we are unwilling to change ourselves. It is because we are what we are that we have the displeasing conditions. Without changing ourselves—meaning our way of thinking, our desire-patterns, and our unreasonable self-demands—we are doomed to continue writhing in the quicksand of our own endeavours.

How we love our suffering! We are willing to give up anything but the comfortable habit-patterns that are causing our misery. We will not throw away our crutch. Assuming we are the "good guys," that we are looking from the highest possible peak, we rationalize and see our present situation as other than what it is. We want the rose without the thorn and the joy of autumn without the cold of winter.

Look in the mirror closely—what do you see in the face there? Be honest. Is there compassion, joy, energy, and good health, and a picture of fulfillment? If not, obviously something is wrong, isn't it? Perhaps we do not have the intelligence to ingest the teachings of the greatest sages, so we must introspect at our own levels in order to comprehend what is wrong and what must be done. Being undisciplined, we postpone such a step indefinitely, and this is suicide—literally, self-death. Heart attacks, strokes, ulcers we take as the natural consequences of living. By then it may be too late. Paying huge doctor bills as ransom avails nothing.

Without self-culture—physical, mental, and spiritual—we begin to die early, in life and our existence becomes one long death progression. Pretending we are immortal, we ignore the present symptoms and insist our usual way, which led us to the present predicament, is best. If we can truly believe, as the Soto Zen Genjo Koan states, that this world is, just as it is, our ideal state, well and good. Then, of course, there will be no complaining. If, as many pretend to do, we "surrender" to an Oriental teacher, then he is carrying the load and we have abandoned any concern, no matter how things go. If our prayers remain unanswered, we cannot complain because we have "surrendered" to God. But how many actually do so? We depend upon ourselves, not in the best sense (as the Buddha advised), but in the worst way. Dissatisfied with ourselves and our self-made lot, we depend upon our limited being.

When we hate someone, anyone, we cannot love at all. If we place ouselves above others, we cannot see the absolute value of all things. If we do not realize that we exist in total relationship, we are separated from others. And so we grasp only what appears favorable, hoping everything else will disappear. In so doing we divide the Joyous Mountain into plots, and subdivide into "yours" and "mine," "good" and "bad," etc. We live with hypocrisy and find we are unwilling, and not ready, to die. Dying each day, we pretend that death will pass us by. If we cannot appraise our present situation and determine how we got here ('a very concrete "here and now"), how can we face anything as nebulous as death? And yet we will die, and only by tasting death beforehand, often, can we live life. Only what we do not grasp and what can be dispensed with can be enjoyed. We cannot enjoy the "absolutely necessary." Such attachment makes only for the suffering that attends the possibility of losing it, the jealousy, the envy, and the inevitable bitterness inherent in a grasping way of life. And yet, to face death squarely, we need a disciplined mind.

The Fasting Mind discards as it grows. Wanting to possess nothing, we have everything, as St. John of the Cross pointed out. Retrogressing from the habitual to the spontaneous and from the artificial to the natural, we eventually arrive at our place of origin, the spiritual heart. "Losing a little each day," we stand firm in an inner relationship with sky and earth, relinquishing all and gaining nothing. This is not a prospect that lures the fool. Meditation is hard work and promises no material reward. Introspection is painful, so why do we do it? Because, without finding out who and what we are—manifestly "ourselves"—we do not have a chance. We are like the animal that eats poisonous herbs and throws up, only to eat them again and again. Face the fact that we cause our own suffering. Then the rest is comparatively easy; we change ourselves. We think the thoughts and perform the actions that will reflect what we want in the future. Emptying ourselves, we find a quiet joy within. We make every effort not to make any effort. Basking in the sun, breathing in the wind, we lose sight of gain and loss. Can we do it? Eventually we *must* do it. If we want an apple tree, we must plant the apple seed. We cannot expect effect without suitable cause. If we want the serenity of untroubled mind, we do not do away with death or trouble—this is impossible. To live is to have worries, and eventually, to die. We change our attitude toward things, empty ourselves of our previous habitual responses, and, cultivating a new soil ground, find it empty and ready for the new seed. This spiritual seed then makes it possible for us to Climb the Joyous Mountain.

Joy is Man's Heritage

Pleasure is a reaction. You have either just fulfilled some desire, experienced a sensory or psychological gratification, or had some suffering lifted from your shoulders. In each case the pleasure is temporary, and must be renewed again and again if we are to pursue the familiar pleasure-pain syndrome throughout our lives. Where the pleasure has been achieved in an illicit manner, it is an invitation to future pain. Pleasure and pain are the two sides of the same coin, and we cannot eliminate one while we endlessly experience the other. Besides, just as the Chinese Yang eventually turns to Yin, pleasure indefinitely extended becomes pain. To want something and not get it is painful; to acquire it and then worry about losing it, as in jealousy, is even more painful. There is no "up" without "down," and there is no pleasure without pain.

Joy is your natural state, though it is usually clouded over. When the Mind returns to its natural condition, you are joyful. Such Bliss is not the result of anything. "To the Mind that is still the Universe surrenders." The Life Force Itself is joyous; all we have to do is get ourselves out of the way and enjoy it. This is not difficult for animals and plants, but few humans achieve the natural and the spontaneous. As our lives become more and more artificial, we depart from our natural state of mind and become devious, seeking to manipulate what really cannot be manipulated. The search is for ease, and endless inventions lead us in the mistaken search for such ease. We cease to make effort and become totally undisciplined. Granted untold leisure, we make the search for diversion our total goal, hoping thereby to effect a state of continuous gratification where we do not have the pain of facing ourselves.

We search for such gratification in objects and status, just as we search for knowledge by always looking outward. The scientist, with the aid of modern telescopes, pushes the frontiers of the Universe back and back, totally neglecting to ascertain *who* it is that is looking through the telescope. So, in the search for outer knowledge, the mind is clouded over and we lose our natural heritage of Joy. The worship of words and "facts" goes on to the point where we have the radio and television talking to us twenty-four hours a day, stunting our sensibilities with an outpouring of inane language about so-called "news" (any act of the human condition is "news"). Education is envisaged as a storing-up of great masses of words, as though the life experience only exists in terminology. If we cannot define it, if we cannot isolate it in words, it does not exist. Most scholars have reached the point where they seriously believe anything can be achieved with words. The philosophers play intramural games with other other, and the theologians seek to pinpoint that which has not become part of their own existence. God is drowned in a sea of words, often by clergymen speaking of the poverty of the Son of Man while being careful to keep immaculate their $300 custom-made suits. A Sufi teacher wears the rough, mended cotton costume over his Paris clothes, elegant buckled shoes sticking out, incongruously, from under the hybrid costume. All are full of words, though they are not able to teach their listeners to have the electric experience of entering the crucible. We take away the remembrance of words, from sermons and classes, and are lost as to how to implement the experiences we have heard about. Rare is the teacher who leads his pupils to their own experience, giving them the tools whereby they can achieve the disciplined state necessary to allow the Mind to return to its natural condition. We repeat the Mantra of Knowing, as we read it in a weekly magazine, but we do not become the Mantra. Today we are drowning in words. What a blessing it would be to destroy all television and radio sets, to do away with the freeways of the world, and to once more turn back to the Heart of the Universe for our guidance! How many allow themselves the pleasure of hearing the rustling of leaves and the honking of wild fowl? We pay homage to Thoreau, but we follow the example of Babel.

There is usually the excuse that we have no time. But we have made our lives. We can be joyous if we are worthy of it. We must always remember the lesson: without changing the causes, we cannot expect a different result.

CHAPTER 10

WHO AM I?

Not all religious seekers find ultimate answers. Some do, some don't. I'd like to deal with both here. Rabindranath Tagore, the great 20th-Century poet of India, often wrote in English, and he expressed the final bewilderment of those who don't find answers in the following stanza:

"The first day's sun has asked

At the manifestation of new being–

Who are you?

No answer came.

Year after year went by.

The last sun of the day

The last question utters

On the western seashore

In the silent evening–

Who are you?

He gets no answer."

This question, "Who am I?", repeats itself over and over to the introspective mind. If a man has not asked himself this question at some time, and has not even been concerned with the meaning of existence, he has not lived; like an animal, he has eaten and slept, and, perhaps, procreated, but he has made no effort to rise to true Human status. Zen monks have always tried to penetrate the meaning of birth and death. Where there is birth, there is always death. Is there something unborn that does not die?

To those few fortunate ones who have received their answer, it has not come in words. It is an experience that is not describable, and so cannot be transplanted to another.

Perhaps the greatest Saint Japan has known was the 12th-Century Shinran, who was persecuted and, at one time, exiled to remote corners of the islands. Being married, at a time when monks did not wed, he was laughed at by many, but he eventually found his Way in the belief in the Saving Power of Amida, the Buddha of Infinite Light.

During his many years spent in meditation at the Tendai monastery on the top of Mount Hiei, near Kyoto, Shinran found only despair. This was beautifully described by his grandson, as follows:

"Many moons passed as he practised contemplation on the moon of the three-fold truth in the ten-stage meditation, and the seasons' flowers renewed their fragrance many times as he disciplined himself in pondering on the truth of one hundred words with one thousand modes of thusness. Then he reflected on the problem of emancipation and thought: No matter how hard I try to calm the water of meditation, waves of consciousness arise to disturb it. However hard I try to contemplate the moon of mind-nature, clouds of illusion overcast it!"

This, verily, is the description of a Dark Night of the Soul. But, eventually, Shinran stopped trying, stopped using the power of Shinran, and gave himself up to a greater Power, Amida Buddha. Long ago, at a time without beginning, Amida was a Bodhisattva (enlightened being on the way to Buddhahood). At that time Amida made a vow to save all sentient beings, no matter how numerous they might be. That vow is still in effect. Giving up the self-power that had failed, Shinran, through his teacher, Honnen, learned to give way to the Other-Power on Amida, and from then to the end of his life he was serene in the faith that Amida's vow would surely save him. He died repeating the Nembutsu—the short "NAMU AMIDA BUTSU" ("Hail to the Buddha of Infinite Light") that simple believers say over and over each day, knowing that, if they call on

Amida and rest secure in His Saving Power, they will be taken to the Western Paradise. This is called EKO in Japanese, meaning that there is a merit-transference from Amida, who endows us with merit-power by crushing the egocentric and separative self of man. According to Jodo Shinshu Buddhism, constant repetition of the Nembutsu, said with firm faith, assures one of being reborn under ideal circumstances in the Pure Land, from where it will not be difficult, minus encumbrances, to reach complete enlightenment.

This belief in the Saving Power of Amida is, of course, much like what we call Christ Consciousness. There is no doubt such belief alters the level of consciousness, and it may be thought that the Pure Land (Western Paradise) represents this Religious Consciousness brought to a state of maturity.

In his writing called "Jodo Wasson," Shinran graphically shows how he found his way, and how the spector of doubt vanished from his life forever. Simply and powerfully he wrote:

"Unhindered like space in the light cloud,
Free from all impediments,
None is there unblessed by the light.
Take refuge in the Inconceivable One.

Also, he wrote:

"Unequalled is the pure, clear light. When we meet, and trust, this light, all our Karmic bonds are renewed. Take refuge in the Ultimate Resort."

———————————

2500 years ago, Gautama, Prince of the Sakya people in Northeast India, left his future kingdom, his wife and son, to become a homeless mendicant. After wandering, and almost starving, for six years, he realized Perfect Enlightenment and became the only Buddha of Historic Times. He was not a Philosopher or a theoretician. In turning the Wheel of the Law, he tried to show the way for all beings to reach the Enlightened State of a Buddha (Nirvana), and to, thereby, end all Suffering. His was a practical Path of Compassion, and much of what follow refers to his teaching, for he certainly was one who found Ultimate Answers.

Many times we read accounts of fantastic psychic experiences of various seekers and Saints. The uninitiated are fascinated with this razzle-dazzle, mistaking mental aberrations for Enlightenment. In truth, psychic experiences, no matter how desirable they seem, can be hindrances and represent the workings of a mind still bound by delusion. The Buddha told his monks that, if one has total mindfulness of the breathing process, he will see that each simple breath has extension in time—a beginning, middle, and an end. After a while the turn to the next breath will become crystal clear. *Then an experience of a simple mental image, like a star* (usually blue) *will show true Absorption.* Visions and images are indicative of a deluded mind. This will be disillusioning to many, who want to read about, or have, lofty experiences, but it is important for the sincere meditator to remember. And the Buddha said there are five hindrances that interfere with Meditation: sense desire, anger, sloth or torpor, agitation and worry, and doubt.

Meditation enables one to know the mind, and knowing it, to shape the mind, leading to a freeing of the mind. When habit patterns are broken and even the tendencies burned to ashes, there is Freedom and Stillness, but not before. Until this is done, we have a state of mind somewhat like Tagore's, where there are questions and, frustratingly, no answers. When the mind is mastered, whether through the self-discipline of a Buddha or the complete surrender of a Shinran, all doubts vanish and there are no more questions.

This mastering of the mind means mastery of the body. When the body is mastered, said the Buddha, the mind is mastered. The psycho-physical mechanism is one. Enlightenment can be approached through the "physical" side (Hatha Yoga or T'ai Chi Ch'uan) or through the "Mental" (as in Meditation, Japa, etc.)—both are valid. Each time there is a spiritual change, we have a physical change. A man is literally what his Intrinsic Energy (Prana) is. This Life Force changes as we cultivate "ourselves"—and as we cultivate ourselves, the Life Force changes.

— — —

Leading the meditative life, we begin to understand what is meant by the Lotus Sutra (Scripture) when it says:

"From the State of Emptiness, each man's body is a body pervading the Universe, his voice is a voice filling the Universe, and his life is a life which is without limit."

Cultivating this emptiness, meaning to live and act without clinging, without compulsion, and without a seeking heart, is, of course, the task of Zen practisers.

The aim of Zen is to free oneself from all conditions—not to be tied to any condition, however pleasurable, however painful—while living in the midst of conditions. To do this means living in the here and now while transcending the here and now.

Nowhere has the task of Meditation been better spelled out than by the great 20th-Century Sage, Ramana Maharshi, as quoted in the fine magazine of his Ashram, "The Mountain Path."

Bhagavan Ramana said:

"Better than spells of Meditation
Is one continuous current,
Steady as a stream,
Or downward flow of oil.

Better than viewing Him as Other,
Indeed, the noblest attitude of all,
Is to hold Him as the "I" within,
The very "I."

Abidence in pure being,
Transcending thought through love intense,
Is the very essence
Of Supreme devotion.

Absorption in the heart of being,
Whence we sprang,
Is the path of Action, of Devotion,
Of Union, and of Knowledge.

Then Ramana went on to give the following instructions to reach this end:

"Holding the breath controls the mind,

A bird caught in a net.

Breath-regulation helps

Absorption in the heart.

Mind and breath (as thought and action)
Fork out like two branches,
But both spring
From a single root.

Absorption is of two sorts:
Submergence and destruction.
Mind submerged rises again.
Dead, it revives no more.

We may ask of ourselves: How can we "Kill" the mind? How do we give "ourselves" up?

Yet, Chan, Chinese Zen, says: "When nothing remains to give up, one has, indeed, reached the Source."

The principle practice of Zen is, of course, Zazen—the Zen Sitting-in-Meditation.

What is Zazen?

Zazen is NOWNESS!

How does one realize this NOW?

By harmonizing mind and body.

How does one harmonize mind and body?

By forgetting mind and body.

In what way is the self realized?

By forgetting the self, the self is realized.

– – – – –

I'd like to close this chapter by quoting Professor Ogata's fine translation of the famous "Song of Dhyana" by the great Japanese Zen Master, Hakuin Zenji. "Dhyana," of course, is Meditation, so this is the Song of Meditation from a Zen Master, and it never fails to knock me out, whenever I hear it.

"The Song of Dhyana"

ALL BEINGS ARE PRIMARILY BUDDHAS; IT IS LIKE WATER AND ICE:
THERE IS NO ICE APART FROM WATER: THERE ARE NO BUDDHAS APART FROM BEINGS.
NOT KNOWING HOW CLOSE THE TRUTH IS TO THEM,
BEINGS SEEK FOR IT AFAR–WHAT A PITY!
THEY ARE LIKE THOSE WHO, BEING IN THE MIDST OF WATER, CRY OUT FOR WATER, FEELING THIRST.

THOSE WHO, FOR ONCE,
LISTENING TO THE DHARMA,
IN ALL HUMILITY
PRAISE IT AND FAITHFULLY FOLLOW IT,
WILL BE ENDOWED WITH INNUMERABLE MERITS.
BUT HOW MUCH MORE SO
WHEN YOU TURN YOUR EYES WITHIN YOURSELVES,
AND HAVE A GLIMPSE INTO YOUR SELF-NATURE!
THE TRUTH PERMITTING NO IDLE SOPHISTRY.
FOR YOU THEN
OPENS THE GATE LEADING TO THE ONENESS OF CAUSE
AND EFFECT;
BEFORE YOU THEN
LIES A STRAIGHT ROAD OF NON-DUALITY AND
NON-TRINITY.

WHEN YOU COME TO UNDERSTAND
THAT FORM IS THE FORM OF THE FORMLESS,
YOUR COMING AND GOING TAKES PLACE NOWHERE ELSE
BUT WHERE YOU ARE.
WHEN YOU UNDERSTAND
THAT THOUGHT IS THE THOUGHT OF THE THOUGHTLESS,
YOUR SINGING AND DANCING IS NO OTHER THAN THE
VOICE OF THE DHARMA.
HOW BOUNDLESS IS THE SKY OF SAMADHI!
HOW REFRESHINGLY BRIGHT IS THE MOON OF THE
FOURFOLD WISDOM!
BEING SO, IS THERE ANYTHING YOU LACK?
AS THE ABSOLUTE PRESENTS ITSELF BEFORE YOU,
THE PLACE WHERE YOU STAND IS THE LAND OF THE LOTUS,
AND YOUR PERSON, THE BODY OF THE BUDDHA.

There is nothing to be added to this magnificent statement. Can there be any doubt that Hakuin Zenji (who said: "After that, seeing the things of the world was like viewing the back of my own hand") found his answer?

SAINTS AND POETRY

SAINTS ARE NOT POETS BECAUSE
POETS ARE CAUGHT IN THE WEB OF PASSION.
THEY WRITE ABOUT HUMAN SUFFERING,
WHICH THE BUDDHA SAID IS COMMON TO ALL BEINGS.
THE SAGE IS NOT BOUND BY THAT ROPE;
HE HAS REPLACED PASSION WITH COMPASSION,
SO THERE ARE NO POEMS AT HIS FINGERTIPS,
THOUGH THE REAL POETRY,
THE GLORY OF CREATION,
SHINES IN THE CAVE OF HIS HEART
AND EVERY CELL REJOICES IN MUTE TESTIMONY
TO THE LIFE–FORCE
THAT FLOWS THRU US ALL.
SING A SONG OF WONDERMENT!
AND GIVE THANKS, GIVE THANKS, GIVE THANKS.

THE TREES STAND AGAINST THE SKY– – –
SOMETHING IS EXPRESSING.
WHAT IS THERE TO UNDERSTAND?

CHAPTER 11

MONKEYS AND HOLY MEN

Often, while staying on the second floor of a two-family house in Baroda, India, I noticed numerous monkeys outside the window of my room, watching me intently. I asked my host, the student Kaushik, why this was so.

"They are waiting for you to leave your window open when you go out of your room," he replied. "Then they will be able to steal your red umbrella and black hat."

I was astonished. "What could they do with my hat and umbrella?" I inquired, somewhat skeptically.

Kaushik grinned. "Exactly what they've seen you do," he explained. "One monkey will put your hat on his head, and the other will open the umbrella and hold it over him. They are just like men, I tell you!"

This habit of imitation by the monkeys is well known in India, where they relate an amusing story to illustrate it. A hat salesman was traveling through the countryside, going from one town to another. He was carrying many hats, and it was a warm day, so he became quite drowsy. Putting his burden down, he rested his back against a tree and was soon fast asleep, shaded from the noonday sun.

When he awoke some time later, he was dismayed to find most of his hats gone. Looking up, he saw a whole host of monkeys sitting on branches in the nearby trees, watching him—and each one was wearing one of his hats on its head!

He was overcome by despair. "I am ruined!" he thought, but then, knowing of the monkey's propensity for imitation, he conceived a brilliant idea. Putting one of the few remaining hats on his head, he feigned anger, ripped it off, and cast it to the ground with considerable force. Three times he repeated this action, placing the hat on his head and then, in a fit of rage, slamming it to the ground.

The astonished monkeys, seeing this, naturally took the hats from their own heads and, pretending anger, dashed them to the ground, as they had seen him do. He was saved! In a few minutes he had recovered his entire precious stock and was on his way again.

It was Kaushik who told me that, when a monkey grins at you, baring his teeth, he is angry. This bit of information came in handy at a later date. By then I was at an Ashram in the foothills of the Himalayas. One day, walking up from the stony beach of the Ganges, I noticed what looked like a convention of monkeys meeting on the side of the hill. One fellow sat up front, as though addressing the others, and all seemed quite intent on their meeting. I was fascinated, and walked closer to get a better view. The monkeys, noticing the intruder, turned toward me and seemed to grin amiably. Then I suddenly remember Kaushik's warning. Not wanting to be set upon by 75 or 100 simians, I turned and beat a hasty retreat. Obviously it was no time to be curious and break in on their meeting.

I remember an interesting encounter, between several small monkeys and a pack of wild dogs, that took place under the suspension bridge of Laksmanjula, near Rishakesh, a great place for Holy Men in the foothills of the Himalayas. I had been walking with one yellow-robed Sanyasi under the large clock that dominates the town, trying not to notice his occasional excursions to various vendors, from whom he bought a cigarette at a time. He was neither supposed to smoke nor handle money, but this was not my concern.

Hearing some unusual sounds coming from the entrance to the bridge, and noticing a crowd gathering there, I took advantage of my companion's brief absence to walk down and see what was happening. Apparently a pack of wild dogs, catching a monkey mother and her tiny offspring far from any trees, had forced them up the guard rail of the imposing suspension bridge. There the mother and baby rested, and would have been all right if a larger male monkey, perhaps her mate, had not come along and begun to berate the poor mother. She had enough problem taking care of her offspring and evading the wicked-looking dogs without having to fight off the new intrusion. When the larger monkey began cuffing her angrily, she let go of the baby and pushed him up the cable. The tiny tot climbed laboriously, sometimes swinging 360 degrees around, but not letting go. Down below, the pack of dogs waited eagerly for the young one to fall, as seemed inevitable. The Holy Men, in loin cloth or saffron robe, watched in amusement and interest. None would interfere in the drama, however.

Somehow, the mother pacified her mate and he went away. Then she climbed the cable to reach her baby, who had, miraculously, disappointed the waiting dogs below. Reaching the little one, she tucked him to her breast and began her descent. Now she had one problem left—how to evade the dogs and make her way to a tree, or some other shelter, where she would be safe. It was obvious this would not be easy, particularly with the burden on her chest.

Coming as close as she could to the dogs without allowing them to reach her, she began a series of feints. Each pretended movement brought a howl from the dogs, who immediately dashed in the intended direction. It seemed obvious the monkey mother had the superior intelligence. We all waited for her to make her move.

Finally, one time, she felt the dogs were diverted enough to give her a chance. Quickly she dropped to the ground and dashed in the opposite direction, toward a nearby building. The tricked pack of canines came roaring after her, and it was touch-and-go—but she made it to the building and quickly scampered to the roof, just a few feet ahead of her pursuers. Then, showing a remarkable coolness and arrogant confidence, she leaned over the side of the building, holding herself just out of the dogs' reach. I have often seen monkeys tantalizing wild dogs in this manner, not escaping to a real safety ledge but teasing the wild animals by just barely eluding their grasp. Occasionally, on a tree, a pursued monkey will casually pick some fruit, or tear off a small branch, and throw it at his tormenters.

I believe we were all happy to see the monkey mother and

her offspring make it to safety. Now the group of observers began to disperse, and I turned slowly back to the clock-tower in the town. As I did so, I noted one Holy Man who had paid absolutely no attention to the excitement, sitting, the whole time, facing the sun in the opposite direction. It was my friend, Maharaj, in a white cotton dhoti.

I crossed to where he was sun-bathing, face up to the sky. "What have you been doing, Maharaj?" I inquired, suspiciously.

He smiled. "I am just sitting here enjoying the sunshine," was his answer, and I believed him. He had not even noticed the commotion. Maharaj was a great meditator, and one who wandered where he wanted. "He is 'free geese,'" explained another Sadhu, enviously. The latter was attached to a Master and could only go where his Guru told him to go.

At our Ashram there was only one meal a day, about noon. I had noticed that Maharaj was absent at some meals. When I asked him about it, he shrugged. "If I am deep in meditation at the time, I just wait for another day," he explained, as though a day without food was an ordinary occurrence.

Maharaj usually meditated for four or five hours at a time. He seemed relaxed and happy, and I admired him. Years later, I heard he had gone to Canada, where his warm personality attracted quite a following. He taught meditation to many, and was known to have initiated hundreds. Then, suddenly, he was asked to leave Canada within 24 hours. The government had heard that one of his initiates had become pregnant. It was even rumored that he initiated in the nude.

I do not know why the Canadians were so up-tight about the pregnancy. Many Indian Rishis (Sages) had had wives, and the Indian Mythology is full of meaningful sexual encounters. Does not the great "Ramayana" revolve around such a matter? At any rate, it may have been Canada's loss when Maharaj left so abruptly. I do not know where he is these days, but he is probably "just sitting and enjoying the sunshine" somewhere, oblivious to monkey fights and monkey flights, and smiling in the serenity of a peaceful mind.

Early summer evening in a small town has great charm for me. Dinner is finished and dishes put away; there is still an hour or so of daylight in which the young ones can ride their bikes and the older people, basking in the warmth of a comfortable dinner, sit swinging on the porch, or rocking back and forth somewhat noisily in ancient rocking chairs. Fathers are playing on the lawns with their tiny daughters, trying not to feel disappointment that the darling little ones will really never be much fun to play ball with. The cool breeze of evening greets the departing day for all.

This is almost my favorite time, but I like even better the very early morning, just as the sun rises. Those few who have to be up and out so early greet each other almost as conspirators as they feel the freshness of the new day, well repaid for the early chill they felt as they somewhat protestingly left warm beds. It is an hour at which all things seem possible.

I sometimes think we forfeit these moments when we live in a large city.

CHAPTER 12

PROVINCIALISM

"Provincialism" seems to be the most Universal characteristic, as far as I can tell, even supplanting "greed" for the number one spot. It isn't that we each think ours is the best way of life; we usually believe that ours is the *only* way of life. So the Indian—and the Arab man—wear a funny "bedsheet" for clothing. It never occurs to Westerners that, if they lived in such a hot climate, they, too, would find it rewarding to wear loose-fitting white "dresses" rather than pinched-in uncomfortable trousers. The modern Japanese businessman wears western-style suits, with the usual ridiculous tie, to work, but he often changes into traditional loose kimono when he arrives home; he feels more comfortable in the latter, while wearing the former for show. Actually, daily costume depends upon geography and climate. The nomadic Mongolian people wear the same heavy outer clothes the year round; in the cold weather, they keep out the chill, and, in the warm summers, they protect the body from the outer heat. Those who live in extreme tropical climes keep the windows closed as much as possible to keep the hot air out. Each learns to adapt to his environment. So, why do we in the West feel amusement when we see Arabs on television? We compare their garments with our ridiculous way of dressing (in hot, humid weather the woman wears almost nothing and the conforming man must have on a suitcoat and choking necktie) and, since we are the judge and jury, find their practical adaptation amusing.

We tend to judge people in the same way, trying to estimate how much they differ from the provincial standard set up in our localities. Actually, each one of us is part of a minority; everyone is outnumbered. And no-one ever thinks the other fellow is the "good guy"; after all, it's taken for granted we're the "good guys."

If we live in the suburbs, we try, ourselves, to conform to the group ideal in every way lest our neighbors somehow get the idea we don't belong. Of course, if we are pig-headed, have a feeling for all peoples (not merely our own), and have some peace and inner security (a Spiritual base), we don't give a fig for such judgments. Then we are eccentric, unless we are wealthy and can set our own standards. What a narrow life we tend to live in our suburban communities, where we have huddled together with others who have (or pretend to have) the same means and are devoted to the same group mores! "She has very good taste," we say, meaning her likes and dislikes conform to our own. This is natural, as she has been shaped in the same aseptic crucible as ourselves. Even protest meetings, such as anti-war gatherings, are peopled with others who have the same viewpoint. We don't want dissidents, and assume that everybody in the group votes the same way, reads the same books (if they read at all), and stands for the same type of thing, generally. This despite the fact that the only way such protest meetings could expand our horizons would be if we heard all opinions, contrary and agreeable, together. "I do not agree with what you say, but I will defend with my life your right to say it," from the writings of Voltaire, is not the statement of a provincial man; most of us may agree with his words in principle, but we do not practise what they say.

"My little group is the center of the Universe, and all others must be judged by how they compare to it" is the usual thought. One Asian boy walked away from me in disgust when I tried to describe how trains enter New York City underground. He had asked a perfectly reasonable question, how railroad stations in the large cities of the world compared with that of his own small town, but obviously I didn't take it seriously and offended him by spouting some nonsense about the trains entering a city underground! This was not possible from his point of view; it was not in the ball park with any norm he may have set up.

One time, in Hong Kong, some other travelers and I rented a large car, complete with driver, to leisurely tour the extensive New Territories. They extend to the Chinese border and are leased to Hong Kong for a long period of time, fulfilling well their task of supplying all kinds of food to the gourmet restaurants, as well as the popular street-stalls, of that most crowded of cities.

Near the loosely guarded border we were surprised to come upon a walled village. Only Chinese lived there, and many animals seemed to share their shelter with the people in the mild California-like Canton climate. Adults were going about their work in a busy fashion, and the children were having a hilarious time. Little ones, wearing only tops, no bottoms (I have seen this so often in India and other Asiatic countries, where the small child has nothing in the way of his excreting wherever he happens to be, a very practical arrangement) were chasing chickens and other fowl and running about the countryside in what seemed to be riotous, and gleeful, good health.

An old German woman in our party clucked sympathetically. "Oh, those poor children!" she exclaimed, from a warm and misguided heart. "They'll never have a chance to get anywhere, to amount to anything!"

I was astounded, never having seen healthier babies in my life. "Exactly where would you like them to get?" I asked sardonically. But, of course, she meant they would never have the chance to enter the status struggle in Europe, which was the criterion by which she judged. The fact that the young ones seemed happier and healthier, with fewer discernible hangups, than the children she sees at home did not come across to her. They would never lead "her" life, so, naturally, they were to be pitied.

Another time, staying at Clarke's hotel in Benares (now Varinasi) in India, I met a staid English couple traveling for the first time; the man had just retired from business, and they were beginning to see the world.

Thinking to be a help, I arranged for a young friend of mine, a student at the famed Sanskrit University, to guide them on a tour of what can only be called a Casbah-like neighborhood. Here, under overhangs that kept most of the streets dark, were thieves and pickpockets, beggars and Holy Men, camels and goats, numerous temples with ringing gongs and chanting Priests, and the accumulated filth of thousands of years. It was a fascinating place in the Holiest and most interesting of Indian cities.

When they returned from what had evidently been an extended tour, they were not smiling at all. Indeed, both faces looked tight-lipped and grim, not at all as if they had enjoyed themselves.

"Those poor, starving people!" exclaimed the English woman. "So hopeless, so pitiful . . . " She had noticed none of the interesting sights, only the beggars and mendicants.

"Wait a minute!" I interrupted. "Did you notice the faces on those 'starving' people?"

She said that she had.

"Did they seem any more miserable than the faces you are used to seeing in London every morning?"

She thought for a moment, and perceptibly brightened. "You know," she said, "I was astonished that the filthy beggars seemed so cheerful! After all, what have they to be cheerful about?"

This made me laugh. "And are all your friends in London that cheerful?" I pressed on.

They looked at each other, and then slowly shook their heads. Incomprehensibly, starving people were cheerful, and the 'fortunate' ones they knew back home often wore dour expressions in the morning.

"To be helpless is to often be cheerful," I explained, but they looked dubious. "When there is nothing to strive for, we relax and let our destiny take its course. In India, the workings of Karma, each man's self-made Fate, are well understood. Why should we resent what we have brought on ourselves?"

This was too much for them to handle, so they retired to their room to rest and speculate about the disgusting things they had seen. After all, such dirt was decidedly un-English!

— — — — —

In Benares I had taken a pre-dawn boat trip along the Ganges, past the ghats where newly dead bodies were burning, and through the waters where the incredible sight of so many pilgrims bathing in the sacred waters, seeking absolution, was overpowering. My companions were the young Sanskrit University student and an old middle-European woman I had met on shipboard. When we finally debarked from the boat, as the rising sun began to stream across the sacred river to the chanting of the Gayatri Mantra and other tradition hymns to the Divinity in the Sun, we walked up some narrow alleys to a Nepalese temple seldom noticed by foreigners. The student wanted to show us the sculpture on the outside of the temple, the various statues being graphic enough to bring blushes to even a hardened Parisian's cheeks.

If one does not realize that the explicitly sexual sights really represent the two sides of Reality–Shiva, the imperturbable Destroyer, and his Consort, Shakti, the Power that brings the world into play–the voluptuous sights may well be dismaying, as they were to the European woman. We walked around the outside to inspect the fourteen statues that showed the progression as a man with one wife chose a second–and then the delights of such intimate connubial bliss, graphically portrayed by the artist–until the European woman begged off and refused to continue. She was shocked by what she had thought to be a "Holy" place. It certainly didn't fit her concept of spirituality, and she asked to leave (Japanese visitors always seem turned off by such view in India). There was nothing she could relate to, at all.

Later, the student gave me fourteen photos he had surreptitiously taken of the progressive stages, pictures which were, of course, forbidden. I subsequently carried them out of the country. They are interesting, and could double as naughty postcards, but they do have deep meaning to the Indian people. I have often wondered what the effect would be if I included these photos, untouched, in one of my books.

– – – – –

By an incredible coincidence, I later met the middle-European woman in Africa, at the East African port of Djibouti. I was in a shop trying to understand the intricacies of old French francs, new French francs, and Djibouti francs, when she spotted me. A warm "hello" and she told me that she and her three female friends wanted to shop in the Arab section of the city; would I like to come along?

I looked at my watch dubiously. It was almost noon, and I knew that, after lunch, the people in such African towns take a siesta until the heat of the day wanes, sometimes as late as 5 P. M. "How about this evening, after dinner?" I suggested tentatively. She shook her head – they had to be back on the dock by 4 p.m. or they'd miss the launch to their boat. And they were determined to shop in the Arab quarter!

I asked them to meet me in an hour, and I would see what

could be done. Against my better judgment I made some inquiries, and finally found an official who thought he could "persuade" a particular Arab trader to open for a little while after lunch. He told us to meet him on the corner of Place Pigalle (honestly!) by a building called "the Ritz" at 1:30, when practically everybody would be taking his siesta.

It was really hot, and getting hotter, when we followed the the official through the white-walled streets (deserted, and rather sinister-appearing) of the Arab quarter. Two men were dozing on some steps, shielded fromthe sun, and they were evidently waiting for us. Neither of them showed any enthusiasm about opening up, and they spoke not a word, though I am sure they anticipated several big sales on this particular occasion.

The stock of the store was not overly interesting, but there were some good bolts of material and odds-and-ends of value. Silently the owner—and his assistant—showed whatever was requested. Thirty minutes passed in this way; three quarters of an hour, then an hour went by uneventfully. I could see the owner begin to fidget, used as he was to sleeping at this hour. Suddenly it came to me that these women were only looking, that they had no intention of buying anything! At that moment I wanted to be anywhere else but in that same Arab quarter.

Almost two hours after we arrived, we exited into the broiling sun, the women thanking the two traders graciously, and the latter brooding with thoughts only too obvious to read. I was sure there was no danger, but I did not want to be in that corner of the city again during my stay!

— — — — —

Inexplicably, the European woman had decided to miss the launch that night and stay in town at a place that rented rooms. She asked if I would accompany her to a Camel auction. This sounded interesting—I hadn't known about—and I agreed, though I knew it would be rather difficult to find a taxi at that hour.

The Somalis—for this was French Somaliland—are handsome people, tall, cafe-au-lait in color, and very much at home in the French language. They look much like the attractive residents of

Trinidad in the Western hemisphere.

Entering the huge grounds of the Camel auction, we were almost blinded by the sunlight. There was great activity, even at that hour of the day, and it seemed as though every camel in Africa was there waiting to be sold. Camels have a grieved and complaining look, which is probably justified. Though they are asked to carry huge loads, they are really delicate-looking animals. Most of those at the auction grounds were kneeling in the hot sun, the front two legs carefully hobbled, waiting till it was their master's turn to offer them to the assembled crowd of buyers and onlookers. The stench was particularly strong.

One tall, handsome young man—really a Belafonte type—smiled brightly at us as though he recognized us, and walked swiftly in our direction, hand outstretched and uttering greetings. My companion did not understand French, and she shrank back in alarm.

"He just wants to touch you and be friends," I explained in English. The young man looked hurt. I joked with him a moment, and then he smiled. Finally he was able to ceremoniously shake hands with both of us.

We were near the auctioneer, and soon we saw a little drama. It became the opportunity of one camel owner to bring his animal to the auctioneer before he was ready. He had been daydreaming, and, suddenly made aware it was his turn, he shouted at the animal and began beating it with a stick. Resting on the knees of its front legs, hobbled, the animal tried to lunge to its feet, but could not do so. The owner beat the poor beast furiously, and it made piteous grunting noises as it tried to get off its knees, but he had forgotten to loosen the hobbles. I was afraid the Camel would break both of its thin legs on his desperate effort to rise.

My woman companion stood open-mouthed, and then began to cry. She turned to me. "Make him stop beating that poor animal!" she pleaded in her gutteral English.

"Who, me?" was my incredulous thought. 5000 Somali camel-drivers on those grounds, and she wanted me to interfere! Still, I did feel for the Camel—and all the animals and owners out in that hot sun. Instead of saying anything, however, I put my arm around her to comfort her. And then, fortunately, the animal successfully lurched to its feet, the owner noticed the hobbles and released them, and the little drama was concluded.

Later, the spell of the star-filled sky over the placid waters of the harbor, the sound of distant music, and the light of the incredibly large moon filled me with the wonder of Africa. Arab traders, raucous camel drivers, and lovely dusky ladies were mixed in my thoughts, and underneath the thinking mind something buzzed and revolved and told me I was alive.

EPILOGUE

The world is a reflection of ourselves. What we see without is an accurate measure of what we are within. If there is serenity inside, the world outside seems friendly. When we go to a strange place with our hands outstretched and open, willing to offer whatever we have to give, the reception is warm, we make friends, and life is joyous. But, if we grasp, if we go to manipulate and exploit, the result is different. Our vibration is changed, our appearance is uninviting, and we repel others.

The mind that is often in meditation carries within it a continuous current of livingness, perhaps best described as "suchness." We cannot pretend serenity; it will show in the way we meet daily situations. Each event, each meeting, has its own value, if we can appreciate it. And the Way of Heroes is the quiet way.

What technique of meditation we use, if we do meditate formally, is not important. Expanded awareness, or an inner certainty, are the fruits, and they do not have to be explained. "Know Thyself" is only possible when we go within and probe the deepest levels, far beyond the conscious, thinking mind. To rest in awareness, without labeling each happening "good" and "bad," "pleasing" or unpleasing," takes training. The mind is restless with the habit energies of many life-times. These are well-worn grooves that we follow habitually, just as we speak our native language. To learn a new tongue is difficult, and to go in new directions is also hard. If we do not make the effort, we stagnate. Habit is man's greatest enemy, spontaneity a great boon. The mind conditioned by meditation does not have to pause for long reflection; the reaction is instant, and often we hear ourselves saying something meaningful and think: "Did I say that?"

Perhaps it would be helpful if each teenager, as he reached twenty, spent a year in spiritual training much like that a monk undergoes with a Master. How much more constructive this would be than Military training ("The purpose of a soldier is to kill" I was told my first day in the army)! In olden India a man had three periods in his life: (1) As a student he had a Guru and was expected to follow spiritual practice (2) as an adult he married and became a householder and family man, and (3) at about the age of 50 he distributed his worldly goods and devoted the rest of his life to God, becoming a homeless Sanyasi.

Of course, such a program is not practical today and seldom followed in modern India. I have met those who have tried to follow it, renouncing their families at the age of 50, and they usually have suffered greatly. But, to have one year of monk's training under a true teacher, with no ambition, no competitiveness, would be beneficial for the individual and for all society. The growth from such a year would last a man's lifetime, and perhaps we would come to worship something besides money and status. Such a discipline is particularly needed in Japan, where the old way is rapidly dying and Affluence has replaced the Emperor and the Sun-Goddess as object of devotion. Business is competition, and competition is murderous. It is true what the world calls "progress" is brought about by competitive forces, which also spawn war. Scheming is honored and cheating thought to be distasteful only if one is apprehended. Would not the "hopeless" way of the monk and nun, for one year (and perhaps one month every three years thereafter) teach us to have respect for life? How can we respect ourselves if we do not respect others? They *are* ourselves.

A FEW RANDOM THOUGHTS:

We create needs, and then struggle to fulfill them – which is like voluntarily placing our ball in the sand-trap.

– – – – –

Time has always seemed to me to be Expansion and Contraction. This would account for the cyclical nature of events.

– – – – –

Memory cannot be real as it fades and dies. That which perishes is not Real. So Memory is perishable, Reality is not.

– – – – –

The Japanese have their Tea Ceremony (ChaNoYu) as a way to stop the outward flow of everyday life and to introspect for a while. Our way is the Ice-Cream Cone break. Have you ever seen anybody looking unhappy eating an ice-cream cone? Everybody declares a moratorium on worries while he goes thru the ritual of picking THE correct flavor, and then licking it with a conspiratorial air.

– – – – –

What is the sinner who drinks, blasphemes, and has no redeeming feature? He is the teacher of Buddhas!

– – – – –

Only the life based on Truth can bring Ultimate Joy. That life grounded in deception and delusion – no matter how attractive, and how "successful" – ultimately results in great, and continuous, suffering. And yet, there is not one in one-thousand who wants Truth. Mostly, we want to re-affirm our status, like the fat lady who tries ten doctors before she finds one who will recommend a diet with all the foods she likes.

– – – – –

How wise and beautiful the saying of Dogen Zenji, the great 12th and 13th Century Japanese Zen Master:

"Spring draws in flowers and flowers draw in Spring."

– – – – –

I have meditated in the Himalayas, in Zen temples, in the desert, and on distant islands. Best of all, for me, have been periods spent in Absorption under the giant redwoods of Northern California. These are the oldest creatures on earth, and their vibration is powerful for those who will open themselves.

– – – – –

Question: "Why must there be Chinese and Indian, French and English. Why must there be different peoples and wars?"

Answer: (by Zen Roshi Joshu Sasaki, holding aloft his fist and slowly unfolding his fingers): "I have five fingers; why do I have five fingers?"

BOOKS BY JUSTIN F. STONE

T'ai Chi Chih (Joy Thru Movement)
Abandon Hope
Climb the Joyous Mountain
The Joys of Meditation
Zen Meditation
The Metaphysics of Wall Street
Meditation for Healing
20th Century Psalms
Heightened Awareness

two texts and a translation

Justin F. Stone is the originator of T'ai Chi Chih and was formerly a T'ai Chi Ch'uan teacher. From music (where he was an arranger and an A.S.C.A.P. composer), he went to Wall Street where he owned half a seat on the New York Stock Exchange and was advisor to insurance firms, brokerage firms, and others. He then taught at several Universities, invented and taught a language-learning method, became active as a jazz pianist, an exhibiting painter, and a writer teaching Oriental disciplines. He is well-suited to do the latter, having studied and practised extensively in India, Chinese cities, and Japan (where he still stays at a Zen temple occasionally). Justin is also active in presenting seminars in various parts of the country. His poetry, which he considers his best work, is not known.